The Birth of Personality

THE DEVELOPING BODY AND MIND

Series Editor:
Professor George Butterworth, Department of Psychology, University of Sussex

Designed for a broad readership in the English-speaking world, this major series represents the best of contemporary research and theory in the cognitive, social, abnormal and biological areas of development.

The Birth of Personality

The Development of Independent and Moral Behaviour in Preschool Children

Eugene V. Subbotsky
University of Lancaster

HARVESTER
WHEATSHEAF

New York   London   Toronto   Sydney   Tokyo   Singapore

First published 1993 by
Harvester Wheatsheaf
Campus 400, Maylands Avenue
Hemel Hempstead
Hertfordshire, HP2 7EZ
A division of
Simon & Schuster International Group

Typeset in 10/12pt Ehrhardt
by Photoprint, Torquay, Devon

Printed and bound in Great Britain by
Biddles Ltd, Guildford and King's Lynn

British Library Cataloguing in Publication Data

A catalogue record for this book is available from
the British Library

ISBN 0–7450–1468–2 (hbk)
ISBN 0–7450–1469–0 (pbk)

Contents

Contents

Preface

My interest in the problems of personality development in children emerged in 1970 when I was a student at the Psychological Department of Moscow University. Working in the research group directed by Alexander Romanovitch Luria I studied how normal 2–5-year-old children fulfilled the programmes traditionally used as tests for adult patients with lesions of the frontal lobes.

Once I noticed that a 5-year-old boy could not manage the programme that earlier had been handled easily by much younger children. Then I discovered that two small children were conducting the same programme behind my back, whereas my subject was merely imitating their wrong actions. As soon as I isolated my subject in a separate room he shifted to the correct actions that he had been unable to make in the presence of other children.

The case brought me to a simple conclusion: in order that a child can fulfil a programme in a real-life setting he or she does not merely need to know how to do it; he or she should also be able *not* to imitate other people's wrong ways of doing the programme. In other words, the child should possess a particular quality: the ability to display independence regarding other people's actions.

It occurred to me that this ability may be extremely important not only for children, but for adults as well as for society. Even a genius would never openly express his or her innovative views if he or she lacked the courage to oppose the views of traditional theories, in other words, if he or she did not possess independence and 'spiritual courage'.

I became interested in the studies of independence in psychology. I discovered that following the famous experiments by Solomon Asch many scholars had explored 'nonconformity' in children and adults. The studies yielded interesting results. However, all them employed Asch's original experimental method and shared its initial limitation: they studied independence and conformity in the domain of verbal judgements only, and not in the domain of real actions. Besides, the 'confederate group' method was hardly appropriate for studying independence in very young children. This conclusion prompted me to create a different method that would allow me to measure independence and conformity in children older than 2½ years, both in the domain of verbal judgements and in the domain of real actions.

I found that independence, traditionally viewed as an achievement of adolescence, emerges even in 3-year-olds. It is not a unique personality trait, rather, it is a common psychological quality that, to a certain extent, develops in everyone in early childhood. It is the degree or proportion of independence that varies. First, it appears in the domain of verbal judgements, and later in the domain of real actions. Initially, the child is able to reveal independence relating to peers, and then, somewhat later, relating to adults. It was also clear that in order to help the child to become independent it is not enough to teach him or her to be aware of an adult partner's errors; a major obstacle to be overcome is the child's global-imitative attitude (GIA) towards adults as to 'infallible models'. The causes that underlie the young child's global-imitative attitude and the methods that can foster the child's independence in his or her verbal judgements and real actions are described in the first half of this book.

I soon realized that independence is only one aspect of a matured personality. To live in a society an independent individual must respect other people's independence. He or she has to acquire certain intrinsic barriers that could put limits to his or her unbounded self-realization. These intrinsic barriers are no more than interiorized moral imperatives. Therefore, moral development may be viewed as a necessary addition to independence: a socially matured personality can be created only if the two qualities develop side by side, complementing and balancing one another. Thus, the second group of studies appeared – studies of the development of moral behaviour in preschoolers.

Despite the fundamental structural differences between independence and moral behaviour they were found to share certain important features. As with independence, moral behaviour first appears in a young child in the domain of verbal judgements and only later in the domain of real actions. As with independence, true morality is a consequence of an emotionally positive democratic style of social interaction between adults and children. As in the development of independence, a major part of the development of moral behaviour belongs not to cognitive structures but to motivation.

One fact that I discovered in my experiments seems of particular interest: very often children who easily observed moral norms when they were under the surveillance of adults or peers, deviated from the norms as soon as they were left alone in a room. There were, however, children who observed the moral norms even if they had the opportunity to ignore them, e.g if they were sure that nobody would know about their transgressions. Outwardly, the two types of moral behaviour looked alike but their motivational underpinnings were different: in the one case, moral norms were observed because of the external compulsion, in the other case, because of the intrinsic incentives.

Further investigations showed that these two types of moral behaviour (pragmatic and unpragmatic) have different structures and are impelled to development by different causes: if the development of pragmatic morality is based upon the increasing of external control over the children's moral behaviour (which is a characteristic feature of the authoritarian style of social interaction), the development of nonpragmatic morality is fostered by the increasing of the democratic and cooperative style of social interaction between adults and children. It was found therefore that the development of independence and nonpragmatic moral behaviour on the one hand, and the development of conformity and pragmatic morality on the other, may have common psychological roots despite their outward dissimilarity. These and other problems (i.e. parents' concepts about the age of moral responsibility, parents' attitudes towards childrearing practices and children's moral behaviour, etc.) are discussed in the second half of this book.

Last but not least, I always viewed laboratory experiments on personality development as insufficient if they were not tested in practice. Too many worthy psychological studies are buried on library shelves without much hope of being put into practice, although practice definitely might benefit if they were. The only possible way to avoid this fate that I can see for experimental psychologists is to become practitioners themselves, at least for a while. That is why the analytical studies of independent and moral behaviours were supplemented by the extended interventional field studies in which I tried (although with varying success) to develop these qualities in children in real-life settings in classrooms. I suppose that intervention studies of this type might be more helpful for the real classroom practice than the 'pure' experimental studies. Any society, if it is interested in development and not in mere conservation of its structures and institutions, should feel the advantage of having independent and morally educated individuals. That is why I hope that this book may evoke interest not only in developmental experimental psychologists, but in practitioners dealing with childrearing and education in families and primary schools and in social workers and therapists engaged in problems of behaviourial disorders. It might also be interesting for those who create books for children, and for everybody who is not indifferent to the problems of the development of the child's personality.

A number of people contributed to this book either directly or indirectly. I am grateful to all my young subjects, to the students who worked with me in Moscow kindergartens. I remember with gratitude the teachers and educators who helped me in my studies. But my greatest debt is to my teachers, A. R. Luria and A. V. Zaporojetz. I dedicate the book to their memory.

Acknowledgements

Chapter 1: none of the material contained here has previously been published.

Chapter 2: parts of this chapter have appeared in the following journals: 'Communicative style and the genesis of personality of preschoolers', *Soviet Psychology*, 1987, 25, 4, pp. 38–58; 'The formation of independent behaviour in preschoolers: an experimental analysis of conformity and independence', *International Journal of Behavioral Development*, 1993 (in print). The material is reprinted with the kind permission of the publishers.

Chapter 3: parts of this chapter first appeared as 'Development of moral behaviour in preschoolers in a psychological-pedagogical experiment', *Soviet Psychology*, 1981, 20, 1, pp. 62–80; 'Shaping of moral action in children', *Soviet Psychology*, 1983, 22, 1, pp. 3–19; 'Moral socialization of the child in the Soviet Union from birth to age seven', in Roopnarine, J. L. and Carter, B. D. (eds), 'Parent–child socialization in diverse cultures', Norwood, NJ: Ablex, 1992, pp. 89–105. The material is reprinted with the kind permission of the publishers.

Chapter 4: the chapter summarizes the previous three chapters and contains the author's view on the origins of personality development in preschool children.

Chapter 1

General problems of the study

Personality: theoretical perspective

What makes personality a particularly interesting object for psychological study is the fact that it represents an inseparable unity of important practical and fundamental theoretical problems. Education, human communication and psychotherapy may vary crucially in their methodologies and results depending on what personality concept they, explicitly or implicitly, rest on. It seems reasonable to believe that early stages of the development of a matured personality might be an interesting subject of study for developmentalists, both theoreticians and practitioners. Clearly, a psychological theory explaining this development, if it is supported by experimental data, may help in childrearing and educational practice in families and in classrooms. In addition to the tasks dictated by the demands of practice, every science also has another task: that of developing and providing a theoretical foundation for the fundamental concepts that cement this science into a unitary whole and establish its intellectual perspective, for instance, in physics, the concept of an elementary particle; in biology, the concept of life, etc.: in psychology, the personality concept. However, the first question that arises when such a goal is set is about the very concept of personality: what content of an individual can be called personality and what personality can be called a matured one? A brief theoretical analysis of the origins of the concept 'personality' seems, therefore, appropriate before the experimental study can be sensibly and reasonably planned.

In classical thought (Plato and Aristotle), the content that later came to be called the personality was diffusely present in general cosmological concepts of self-movement, the activity of the soul, the mind and life. The tendency to identify the personality with a *causa sui*, perceptible in rough contours in antiquity, was developed further by the philosophy of rationalism.

The foundation of the classical conception of the world and the human being, most clearly embodied in the works of Descartes and Kant, was created by a special intellectual orientation of the postrenaissance thinking towards a critical reconstruction of the world in the forms of human activity. For the rationalist, activity is an experimental, 'practical' endeavour, a way in which the human being understands the world. In the world, 'Reason can see only what it created according to its own plan' (Kant, 1965a, p. 85).

Through this ultimate 'critical attitude' the opposition between the inquisitive human 'I' on the one hand, and 'the kingdom of nature' on the other, was created. The 'I' was invested with such attributes as freedom, spontaneity, activity, morality, responsibility. In contrast, the element of the world of nature (a 'thing') was viewed as lacking all the above mentioned attributes and nature was described as an infinite chain of cause-and-effect relations. Whereas a thing rigorously 'fulfils' the laws of nature and is absolutely passive, an 'intelligent being has a will or a capacity to act in accordance with the idea of laws' (Kant, 1965a, p. 250). Scientific cognition establishes itself as a method for studying nature and determining cause-and-effect relations among the data of sensory experience. Since the human being is a 'corporal creature' and as such belongs to the world of nature, studying it with the tools of science is analogous to studying a thing, i.e. situating it in a natural chain of causal relations.

But the human being is also an intelligent being and as such belongs to the realm of freedom. Freedom makes the human being, in contrast to a thing, an 'end in itself', or a 'person'. It is no accident that Kant used the term *person*, or *personality*, whenever he spoke about freedom. Thus, in the classical sense of the term, the personality is the centre of free creative activity, and any free activity is a personal act.

It is clear that the classical division between the 'I' and nature creates no obstacles for natural sciences, such as biology or physiology, in their studies of the human body. However, it does create a fundamental obstacle for social sciences (for psychology, in the first place), since neither the personality nor its activity can be viewed as causally determined and, therefore, able to be studied by scientific means based upon permanent relationships between stable objects, logical models and calculated predictions. The fact that the human being possesses a personality and freedom of action is an *empirical fact* which, however, is not subject to theoretical explanations. In his *Critique of Pure Reason* Kant demonstrated the impossibility of a 'rational psychology' that claimed to acquire knowledge about the 'I' (or the 'self'). Where there is no place for the laws of nature, there can be no explanation. In the classical conceptual schema, only an empirical psychology that studied the human being (and his or her subjective experiences) as a part of nature, i.e. as a thing, was possible.

This classical division of the 'cognitive space' into two parts, namely, the 'I' (a domain of morality, laws, faith and fine arts) and nature (a domain of natural sciences) has always been a major obstacle for the social sciences in their attempts to locate themselves in the 'file of knowledge'. But nowhere was the problem of 'marginality' so obvious as in the empirical studies of personality since, in a sense, they were the studies of something that escapes causality and explanation. The classical vision of science can still be traced in contemporary studies on personality.

The analysis of the concept of personality in psychology requires that two aspects be distinguished: the structural and the dynamic. There are two 'scales' on which conceptions of the personality in contemporary psychology may be arranged regarding its structure. The opposition between *integrative concepts* (e.g. the personalistic psychology of Allport, 1938) and theories that *delimit the sphere of the personality as some special psychological reality* (represented, for instance, by Lewin, 1935; Cattel's factorial theory, 1957; the 'role theory' of Moreno, 1946; psychoanalytically oriented theories of personality, such as theories produced by Freud, 1966; Adler, 1929; Horney, 1950; Lacan, 1979; Fromm, 1961) is quite evident. A second scale is the opposition between substantialist and nonsubstantialist concepts. The former presents the personality as a certain, stable structure, as a 'system' whose functioning can be studied by scientific means, and be predicted and shaped. These theories include Allport's personalistic psychology, as well as behaviouristic approaches (Eysenk, 1970; Skinner, 1971), 'role' approaches (Moreno, 1946), cross-cultural approaches (Kardiner, 1946; Linton, 1959; Mead, 1970), and the psychoanalytical perspective (Freud, 1966; Adler, 1929; Horney, 1950; Lacan, 1979; Fromm, 1961). The opposite pole is the existential approach (May, 1969) according to which the personality is not something stable and constant, but the capacity of the person continually to go beyond his or her limits through a permanent, never-ending loss of previous structures, towards creative self-construction.

From the dynamic perspective, there is a clear difference bewteen the naturalist and existentialist approaches to the 'sources' of the development of personality. In the former, the process of the development of personality is seen as being wholly made up of the interaction between forces of a biological nature and social environment (behaviourism, factorial theories, personalistic psychology, psychoanalysis). In contrast, those who uphold an existentialist approach see the personality as a *causa sui*, as a self-determined entity (Sartre, 1957, 1966; Camus, 1942; May, 1969).

In my view the attempts to resolve theoretically the controversy between 'freedom' and 'causal determination' in human behaviour cannot be productive since they involve a vicious circle: one fundamental notion (i.e. 'freedom') cannot be reduced to (or deducted from) its conceptual opposition (i.e. causal relationships) simply because each of the two is dependent on the other. The relationships between freedom and causation in human behaviour, which constitutes the 'realm of personality' belong to the same class of problems as the relationships between mind and body, or between retinal projection and perceptual image. Although these relationships exist as empirical facts, they are of correlational and statistical nature and cannot be comprehended as tied by causal connections. If the relationships are described as 'scientific problems', i.e. the subject for explanation, they turn to be 'fundamentally incomprehensible', and even when given an illusory explanation they do not become more lucid since the 'explanation' always comes across some empirical fact it cannot explain. Fortunately for the social sciences, the number of such 'fundamental incomprehensibilities' is very small.

In so far as the personality concept involves the controversy between freedom and causation, an empirically oriented scholar is faced with the option of either accepting one part of the controversy as a basis and denying the other, or accepting the controversy as an existing fact without trying to find its theoretical solution. The first choice brings the scholar to the extreme positions of existentialism and behaviourism, to Sartre and Skinner, to either a sophisticated description of cases in which the 'fundamental choice' is made, or a deterministic explanation of all human actions without application to the 'fiction of freedom'. The second choice gives the scholar an opportunity to explore empirical conditions (such as educational methodologies, subject's social position, social expectations, subject's prior experience, bodily states, etc.) under which subjects most frequently act in this or that way in situations of free options (such as, for instance, to act morally or immorally). However, a theoretical uniformity of explanation falls victim to such a choice, since, on the one hand, all the relationships between the conditions and the subjects' actions can only be statistical and lack the predictive power of a scientific law, and on the other hand, the subjects' actions cannot already be viewed as totally free.

Having said this, I have to acknowledge that it is the second choice that underlies the methodologies of the studies described in this book. It did not seem to me that there is 'utter truth' in either of the two positions implicated in the first choice, although each of them has certain merit. It is equally unfruitful to limit a notion of human personality by reducing it to a group of certain unchangeable 'behaviourial laws', or to view it as a permanent change in which no laws and regularities can be detected. The optimal way for an experimental psychologist to view the personality is as a structure that includes both a compulsory element (coming, for instance, from cultural influences and education) and an element of freedom and unpredictability. Moreover, I think that most of the empirical studies on personality were based on this assumption, explicitly or implicitly, and this book will not be an exception.

Independence and morality as two aspects of a matured personality

However, even if this view is accepted, it is the answer to only one of two aspects, that is, the dynamic one. The problem still remains: what qualities (capacities) should the structure of personality include? Since there are no certain a priori criteria for the determination of these qualities, their number and names vary dramatically, from several to thousands (Allport, 1938). In addition, such pluralism is unproductive since it gives researchers no means for determining priorities and organizing a focused experimental study of personality.

A more productive solution seems to be a position in which a distinction between the personality and the individual is drawn (Leontiev, 1977). Whereas the individual can comprise any (and a potentially infinite) number of 'features' and 'qualities', the personality is a term that includes only the essential features (Ilienkov, 1979). Not every hierarchical structure of individual psychological qualities and capacities can be called a personality, even if it is 'socially typical' and most often represented in the population. Rather, a personality can only be a structure that in a unique way embodies the *universal qualities* in a human being.

Comparing this position with that of Cattell and Eysenk and with other classical Western theories of personality one can see that whereas the latter include in personality a variety of qualities without distinguishing essential qualities from less important (individual) ones the former makes this distinction a central point in outlining the range of personality traits. This position concords with the long tradition of European philosophy of the individual in which the terms 'person' and 'personality' have usually been linked with 'freedom', 'morality', 'responsibility', etc., i.e. with the most essential characteristics of a human being (see Subbotsky, 1987). However, there is still a variety of options about what should be viewed as 'essential' and what should not.

Thus, in some Western studies the 'multidimensional' approach to personality has been replaced by a more focused analysis of certain particular types of personalities, be it the 'authoritarian personality' (Adorno *et al.*, 1950) or personalities with open or closed beliefs systems (Rokeach, 1960) – the priorities mainly inspired by the writings of Fromm (1941) and Maslow (1943). Interest in these particular personality qualities obviously stemmed from the political cataclysms in Europe at that time; if a different starting point were taken, priorities for the selection of 'essential qualities' would be different.

One possible criterion for the selection of the essential features may come from the needs of a particular culture and society. In contrast to many 'traditional' cultures which were oriented mainly on the reproduction and conservation of already existing structures, cultures of European origin have usually been oriented towards expansion and development (see, for instance, Mead, 1970). It is reasonable to assume, therefore, that in European cultures those capacities of the individual that help society to develop must be considered essential. Indeed, looking at the qualities which are usually described as personality qualities we can easily distinguish those that are oriented towards the destruction of existing structures (aggression, emotional instability), or to their conservation (qualities tied to reproductive behaviour), from those that can help to *develop the existing structures*, creativity being the most important of them.

However, creativity is not a characteristic of personality as such, rather, it is a complex quality that includes both cognitive and motivational characteristics. As for the cognitive aspects of creativity, there is a special domain of studies on the problem (see, for instance, Albert, 1990; Crittenden, 1990; Gardner, 1988; Isaksen and Murdock, 1990; Tegano and Moran, 1989). What is interesting for me here is not creativity itself but its social and psychological prerequisite – independence. Since any creative act is normally in confrontation with traditional views, the creator must be able not only to produce new kinds of knowledge and behaviour but to *express that knowledge and behaviour openly and be able to overcome the inevitable resistance and opposition from the conservative side of society*. It is just this ability (or the special sort of 'courage' that enables the creator to follow his or her own ways in thinking and behaviour against the resisting social environment) that will be referred to by the term 'independence' in this book.

Although this way of viewing the term 'independence' may seem rather unusual, it is not the author's invention. The term 'independence' stands for 'nonconformity' in the classical study by Asch (1956) – the ability of a subject to rely upon his or her own opinion with respect to relevant information about the world and not upon opinions of other people that may be distorted by social prejudices or popular beliefs. To employ another well-known distinction between the open and closed systems of beliefs (Rokeach, 1960), it can be assumed that to a certain extent (but only to a certain extent) an independent individual is an open-minded individual in contrast to the closed mind of a conformist. Independence (in the form of 'autonomy of judgements' and 'detachment from culture') can also be viewed in terms of 'psychological health', as an essential characteristic of 'self-actualizing' people (see Maslow, 1954).

One thing that should be pointed out here is that independence is not viewed in this book as a personality trait; it is viewed as a characteristic that every individual possesses to a certain extent and the difference between individuals across the 'independence vs. conformity' scale is not an absolute but a relative one.

Obviously, independence may be beneficial for both the individual and society: it may give the individual a feeling of significance and self-realization; for society it produces new models of thinking and behaviour from which those can be selected which are appropriate for development.

It can also be assumed that from being a productive power, independence, nevertheless, can turn into a destructive power if it goes beyond certain limits. Indeed, independence (and creativity) in its own right does not have a warning signal that can keep an independent individual within those limits and can force him or her to respect the independence of other people. For this to be possible, the independent individual should have certain *intrinsic barriers* that could prevent his or her development into a 'superhuman creature'. These intrinsic barriers are provided through moral norms that, if they are interiorized, create a psychological motivation for moral behaviour.

Morality, therefore, may be viewed as a necessary counterweight to independence; it is a capacity that allows an independent person to make his or her creative contribution without this being an unbounded self-realization of the individual at the expense of other people. Thus, *we can see that independence and morality compose a certain unity directed towards the development of the individual and the society.*

Traditionally, independence and morality have been studied as two separate qualities. In my view, there were two major reasons for this, one based on philosophical grounds and the other on the requirements of empirical methodology. Philosophically, independence and morality belong to different conceptual orientations: independence is a type of individualistic need and is conceivable among other basic needs within the solipsistic (Cartesian) conceptual orientation, whereas moral need can only exist within the 'decentred world' of intersubjectivity in which the existence of other people is acknowledged by a subject as equal in value to the subject's own existence (for the details, see Subbotsky, 1989). From the empirical point of view this separation is justified as well, since independence and morality do not compose a single scale or a unified 'psychological dimension': rather, they should be considered along two different scales (independence vs. conformity, moral vs. immoral behaviour). However, I believe that in a broader perspective the two qualities must be brought together, both in social life and in educational practice.

The reason for this is that both independence and morality are two sides of a single coin – of a matured and socially adapted personality. In a theoretical plane, despite the well-known fact that a direct logical transition from the solipsistic conceptual position to the 'intersubjectivity' position (and therefore, from independence to morality) is impossible (Fichte, 1956), a *real human being* can be identified with neither of these positions, rather, it embraces both of them. To a certain extent every human being lives in a solipsistic world, but in a certain age and under certain circumstances he or she is able to break through the sphere of the 'individual universe' and to join other people (in the act of faith or true moral behaviour, for example) without any 'logical ground' whatsoever. In the area of empirical studies and education, an exaggerated stress on independence or morality alone may well bring about the development of a one-sided individual whose faults may outweigh his or her virtues. On the one hand, a stress upon the development of independence may produce individuals whose unbalanced pursuit of self-realization would permanently conflict with and violate other people's rights. A number of historical examples of the exaggerated development of independence can be found in the epoch of the Renaissance when high creativity and independence (in social life, fine arts, science, etc.) were sometimes accompanied by immoral and even criminal tendencies in one and the same individual (see Losev, 1978). An exaggerated development of morality at the expense of independence, on the other hand, may produce moralistic and dogmatic personalities who are too subject to the existing rules and traditions and too conformist to cope with the changing requirements of reality. Besides, one of the most fundamental requirements of morality is sharing, and the person who is unable to develop his or her own individuality (in the broad sense of the word – including psychological capacities, social position and even economic wealth) has very little to share. It should not be forgotten also that the universal moral values (such as the 'Golden Rule', the Kantian 'categorical imperative', or the moral imperatives of the New Testament) are formulated in a general and unspecified form that allows an individual a rather broad range of actions in which his or her creativity could flourish. There is hardly any need to mention here the numerous examples of such creative innovations in the arts, in science, in religious and social life that changed the face of Europe

over the last few centuries and that were accompanied by a severe
struggle between the new views and ideas and the old and traditional ones.

The last passage should not be taken, however, as the propagation
of a moral relativism. The main characteristic of a matured
personality is just this ability to distinguish between traditions and
views that could (and sometimes should) be violated for the sake of
constructive development and those that should not, to know beyond
which point a development could violate the independence and
universal rights of other individuals.

Of course, a view as broad as that can only be an approximation of
what can be studied in children, especially in preschoolers. In their
early stages of development, both independence and morality only
exist in specific forms. We are not speaking here of independence in
terms of, for example, freedom from conservative views and
traditions; in its original form, independence can only be the
independence of the child from the situational social influences that
contradict the norms and programmes the child has already assimilated and interiorized. However, if this capacity 'to abstain from
global imitation' is developed, it can be generalized later on to
embrace those social influences that are viewed by a young person or
an adult as impeding the development of a certain area of life, be it
science, arts, industry or social relations.

Similarly, moral behaviour of a young child can only embrace the
simplest applications of the universal norms of morality (such as
honesty, justice, fairness, responsibility for one's offences, etc.) to the
child's immediate social relations with his or her peers and close
adults. However, without the child being a good scholar in this
'primary school' of morality, one could hardly expect him or her to
turn into a just and morally sensitive person.

It may be assumed, therefore, that it might be desirable for a
society which is interested in development to produce individuals in
whom both capacities can develop at the same time. Although in their
mature form both qualities can be only developed in a small part of
the population, to a certain extent they must be present in every
normal person, including children. This makes the task of investigat-
ing the early forms of matured personality more feasible. The
problem is now reduced to that of finding adequate methods for
studying the development in children of two universal personality
qualities (or capacities): *independence* and *morality*.

Verbal and actual behaviour as two forms of the development of personality

Earlier we agreed to view personality qualities as relatively stable psychological entities (abilities) that can to a certain extent be objectively explored, predicted and controlled and that display themselves through appropriate behaviours of the individual. In fact, this view is shared by most experimentalists. Traditionally, however, much less attention is paid to the fact that *there are two basic forms of behaviour* that serve as the outlets for personality qualities.

On the one hand, a person can talk about what he or she would do in this or that particular situation, thus revealing his or her personality qualities through *verbal behaviour*. On the other hand, the same person can find him/herself in a real practical situation identical to that represented earlier only in imaginary form. In this case the person has to act practically in order to find a solution and this *actual behaviour* can either be in concordance with the person's verbal behaviour or deviate from it.

Although cognitive components of verbal and actual behaviours are basically the same (i.e. knowledge about the traditional view on a certain problem to which a person found his or her original solution, or knowledge about the moral norms adopted by society), their motivational underpinnings may be substantially different. A characteristic feature of verbal behaviour is that it is 'abstract', 'theoretical' planning and not usually linked with the basic needs of the individual. If the person is talking about his or her assumed actions in an imaginary situation, he or she can easily conform to the requirements and expectations of society (i.e. can say that he or she will be acting independently, will observe moral imperatives, etc.) either to obtain the approval of their immediate social environment or to avoid disapproval. However, when that person finds him/herself in a real-life setting which demands such behaviour, his or her attitude towards it may change drastically. Although the previous motivation (to conform to social expectations) may still be present, new motives may appear. For instance, to really act as a nonconformist the person should have a real (not imaginary) confrontation with an authority figure or with a group of people, to act morally he or she should really have to sacrifice the satisfaction of his or her personal needs, and so on. This new motivation may act against the person's original intention to maintain a socially acceptable way of behaviour and may force the person to deviate from what he or she had been planning to do.[1]

The discrepancy between people's verbal attitudes and their real behaviour has long been studied. In social psychology it was, perhaps, first registered by LaPiere (1934) whose sociological investigation showed the contrast between widespread anti-Chinese sentiments in the US and the actual treatment of Chinese visitors at hotels and restaurants: over 90 per cent of the proprietors indicated in the interview that they would not serve Chinese, whereas in actual fact they all did. The problem was then put in terms of 'validity' of the measures of people's verbal attitudes, i.e. the correspondence between nonverbal and verbal behaviours which many investigators totally ignored (see McNemar, 1946). It was McNemar who first pointed out the correspondence between opinion polls and voting behaviour as a possible case of the practical application of such validity measures. The main difficulty for such a comparison, however, has always been finding appropriate behavioural measures which could be compared with the verbal responses (see Wicker, 1971).

Nevertheless, the social value of determining such measures was acknowledged by many, in particular for the purpose of the prediction of subjects' real behaviour on the basis of their verbal responses (Dollard, 1949). Predictions like that are important, for instance, in childrearing and in social relationships, such as relationships between voters and politicians who may or may not keep their promises if elected. One more example is the problem of to what extent we can expect to have positive results from social intervention programmes which are designed on the basis of verbal responses. A review of empirical sociological and sociopsychological studies showed rather low and mostly insignificant correlations between attitudes and real behaviour, such as individuals' attitudes towards jobs and their real performance or their absences from work, or between people's attitudes and behaviours towards members of minority groups (Wicker, 1971).

Although there is plenty of evidence of the discrepancy between verbal attitudes and real behaviours, the explanation of this discrepancy proved to be a difficult task for the researchers. One possible explanation was the difference between the motives behind verbal and real behaviours: the motives for real behaviour may be stronger than those underlying verbal responses (Deutsch, 1949; Cook and Selltiz, 1964). The other explanation was that the subject was unable to give a verbal response which represented his/her true feelings because of poor intellectual and verbal abilities (Deutsch, 1949; Dollard, 1949).

Many researchers assumed that situational factors may have been a major cause of the discrepancy between real and verbal behaviours (Barker, 1965; Mishel, 1968; Raush *et al.*, 1959, 1960). The assumption that stems from this view is that the more similar the situations in which actual and verbal responses are registered, the stronger the correspondence between them should be. The role of the external control as the possible cause of the real vs. verbal behaviour discrepancy was also mentioned: according to this hypothesis, since real behaviour is normally registered in the presence of other people it may be produced by a subject in order to meet social expectations, whereas verbal behaviour registered anonymously may reflect the subject's real feelings and attitudes (Hyman, 1949; Wicker, 1971). Some evidence on that matter was provided in social psychology experiments (Warner and De Fleur, 1969).

Some other explanations of the verbal vs. real behaviours inconsistency reviewed by Wicker (1971) can be reduced to those already mentioned. Indeed, such explanations as competing role requirements (when a teacher, for instance, behaves in his/her own family contrary to the way he/she teaches his/her pupils to do), availability of overt behaviour opportunities, generality of the verbal responses' objects vs. specificity of the real behaviour's targets, unforeseen extraneous events intervening in the stream of real behaviour, may well be explained by the hypothesis of the different motivational structures of verbal and real behaviours, and the explanation of the discrepancy through expected and/or actual consequences of various acts can be linked to the hypothesis of the role of external social control. Fishbein's three components scheme (attitudes towards behaviour, normative beliefs and motivation to comply with the norms) can also be viewed as a generalization of the previous hypotheses since all three determinants in the final account explain the differences in motivations between attitudes and behaviour. The same relates to the 'theory of reasoned action' (Ajzen and Fishbein, 1980).

In sum, it was concluded that verbal attitudes cannot be viewed as a reliable source for the prediction of people's real behaviour (Wicker,

1971; Tittle and Hill, 1971). It is not my intention here to give an exhaustive account of the studies of relationships between attitudes and behaviour in social psychology (see, for instance, Ajzen and Fishbein, 1980, for such an account). I must note, however, that attempts to overcome the theoretical difficulties which stem from the real vs. verbal behaviours inconsistency, through unification of both types of behaviour in a multidimensional unity (see Rosenberg and Hovland, 1960), do not present a feasible solution since the problem is merely camouflaged. In my view, verbal and real behaviours do constitute two separate levels (or spheres) of human life and not merely two dimensions of one and the same object. Of course, these two levels of life are interconnected, but this connection is more the type of connection between a book reflecting reality and reality itself than a connection between two sides of one apple. Another image of this type of relationship is the relationship between a stage on which a drama of verbal behaviour is being played and the real life that surrounds the stage, or, to put it in metaphorical terms, between the observed observer and the unobserved observer (Goffman, 1982), although sometimes it is difficult to say where the play ends and real life begins (Berne, 1970; Harré, 1979).

The distinction between verbal and actual (real) behaviour has gained a certain recognition in Developmental Psychology as well, for instance in the studies comparing moral judgements and moral deeds (Eisenberg and Miller, 1987; Hoffman, 1988). Although the studies yielded mixed results, they clearly showed the need to distinguish between children's verbal and actual behaviour. Nevertheless, the traditional tendency to give priority to studies of verbal behaviour still prevails. In part, it may be explained by the tradition of Western psychology to make use of questionnaires in the studies of human personality. The preference for questionnaires as measuring instruments in personality studies over observations of a subject's real behaviour was noted long ago (see Corey, 1937; Freeman and Aatov, 1960; LaPiere, 1934) and attributed mainly to the ease of the questionnaire's application as compared to the observation of real behaviour. Although this is, of course, true, the fact of this 'unequal difficulty' needs more elaborate explanation.

It may be assumed that the dominance of the 'verbal approach' in studies of personality stems from the differences between the motivational components of verbal and actual behaviours. The motivation for verbal behaviour can easily be created (through special instructions, rewards and other artificial means) and controlled by the experimenter during the experiment. As a result, subjects' immediate motivation does not even figure among variables in many experiments on personality. Thus, in the projective type of studies the experimenter usually attempts to 'read' the subject's personal motivation from his or her replies to certain standard stimuli, whereas the immediate motivation of the subject who is giving the replies is merely ignored.

With real actual behaviour this cannot be done. In a real practical situation the subject is 'personally involved' and his or her immediate motivation necessarily is an independent variable that influences the behaviour. This motivation can be quite complex, contradictive and not easy to reveal, which is what makes experiments on real behaviour a difficult and time-consuming enterprise.

Nevertheless, it is the motivation of real behaviour in real experimental situations which can bring a scientist the most valuable results, provided that this experimental situation is a model representing a typical real-life situation. Whereas the knowledge of subjects' verbal behaviour has only a remote and indirect relation to how the subjects will behave in a real-life setting, the subjects' real behaviour does provide a reliable means to predict their behaviour in families or in classrooms. It is therefore useful to consider briefly the general procedure for studying the motivation of real behaviour, with special reference to the motivation of a preschool child.

Experimental analysis of motivation of real behaviour in preschool-age children

Normally in real life the 'problem of motivation' appears before the experimenter only in those cases where the subject somehow deviates from the supposed 'optimal way' of behaviour (e.g. from the prediction, partially intuitive, of the experimenter regarding the subject's behaviour). This optimal way of behaviour in each particular situation depends on many factors, not least on cultural traditions, but this conventional expectation is necessary for a normal communication to be possible.

Indeed, if I enter into a communicative interaction with someone (i.e. with a student at school or with a friend, etc.) I expect him or her to behave in a certain way to which I am prepared to react appropriately. In other words, normally I know from experience what my partner is going to feel and what his or her motives are going to be in this situation. If his or her behaviour unfolds roughly in accordance with my expectations, the communicative act proceeds smoothly and brings certain practical results for both of the partners.

There may, however, be cases when the subject's behaviour deviates drastically from what is expected. Since in this case the chain of mutual expectations is broken, the only way to restore it is to determine the causes that forced the subject to deviate. The 'problem of motivation' appears in most real-life situations exactly in this way. For instance, if the child behaves well in a classroom, a teacher and a psychologist are normally concerned with other problems (whatever they are: teaching, communication, development, and so on) than that of the child's motivation. However, if the child starts to reveal systematically aggressive or immoral behaviour, or if he or she begins to imitate any action he or she observes, then the teacher and the psychologist become anxious to find the causes for such behaviour.

For the teacher the reason for this anxiety is usually a purely practical one: he or she has to decide what to do in order to bring the child's behaviour back to normal. For the psychologist, however, this concern may become persistent and grow into a special interest in the motivation which, under normal conditions, makes a child behave in the expected way but then, under different conditions, converts his or her behaviour (and personality) into an aggressive, immoral or conformative one.

What has been said can be illustrated by a simple model. If A and B are the beginning and the end points of a certain behaviourial act, it is assumed here that *there exists a normal (or optimal) way for this behaviourial act to unfold, and this normal way is a social convention that is known to any member of a certain cultural group from his or her social experience.*

I assume therefore that if the subject's behaviour severely deviates from this normal way, a problem 'to determine motivation' (in short, a motivation problem) appears. For a professional psychologist this motivation problem may become a subject matter for his or her studies, thereupon the psychologist will particularly look for children with deviations or will create special experimental conditions in which these deviatory behaviours could be systematically reproduced. A good example here could be Freudian work on the 'psychopathology of everyday life', in which he interpreted the well-known slips (of the tongue, of the pen, etc.) as deviations caused by unknown motivation (Freud, 1910).

The motivation problem in experimental psychology is, however, complicated by the fact that behaviour is a multifactor phenomenon, that is, the combined action of at least three psychological factors (or forces): *knowledge*, *will*, and *motivation itself*. This means that 'behavioural deviation' can be caused not only by (1) some unknown motivation, but also by (2) lack of the knowledge or skills that are necessary for resolving the problem in the supposed 'optimal way', or by (3) underdevelopment of the ability to make the 'voluntary effort' necessary to secure the appointed optimal problem solving. In order to make sure that the deviation is just determined by motivation, one needs at least two control experiments in which knowledge (skills) relevant to the situation and the level of voluntary action development become independent variables. If under one of the conditions the subjects' behaviour in a standard problem-solving situation (the dependent variable) takes the form of the prescribed optimal way (for instance, conforms to moral norms), then the motivational explanation of the deviant behaviour is unlikely.

If, on the contrary, one manages to prove the motivation hypothesis, a new problem might be encountered: how to change the child's motivation in order to make him or her behave in the optimal way? It is not, of course, necessary to complete the motivation analysis by intervention. Sometimes, however, the 'optimal way of behaviour', being the experimenter's cognitive construct, coincides with 'socially desirable behaviour' (for example, with moral behaviour or with 'normal behaviour' in the case of pathological motivational deviations). In this case, the motivation analysis is not an ultimate goal, but rather a way to work out the relevant methods of rearing and correction. If the psychotechnical intervention is adequate, the deviations should disappear.

In sum, the investigation of children's motivation includes three stages: the 'motivation problem' appears before the experimenter when the subjects' behaviour deviates from the expected 'optimal way' of resolving the problem in a standard experimental situation and the deviation cannot be reasonably explained by immaturity of certain intellectual functions or voluntary actions (in short, the problematization stage). The 'motivational-explanation analysis' aims to exclude possible alternative explanations of behavioural deviations: lack of knowledge or capacity to make voluntary efforts (the analytic stage). The psychotechnical intervention is a modification of the children's needs in order to eliminate the deviations (the intervention stage).

This three-stage scheme can easily be applied to traditional studies of motivation that have a long and rich history in psychology (for a review see Ames and Ames, 1989; Maslow, 1954; Heckhausen, 1986). Basically, motivation is viewed in the same way as some elements of the inner or outer world that implement two major functions: they activate an individual and direct his/her activity towards a certain goal. Although the problematization stage in the studies of motivation never attracted too much attention as a special subject for analysis (apart, perhaps, from psychoanalysis, where the search for 'deviations' has been viewed as a special and independent task of analysis – see Freud, 1910), the analytic stage evoked a vast number of studies. The methods developed to determine a subject's motives, although very diverse, can be roughly divided into two major groups. The first group (indirect methods) is based on the 'projection principle' and includes all sorts of interviews, questionnaires, associative techniques, constructive techniques, completion techniques, expressive techniques and, to a certain extent, a psychodramatic method (see Henry, 1960; Rabin, 1986). All these methods are based on the interpretation of the subject's verbal responses and behaviours that are close to them (such as drawing, sculpting, specially organized play, etc.)

A second group (direct methods) is based on the registration of the subjects' real behaviour, either observed in real-life settings or provoked in specially designed experimental situations which represent real-life situations in a laboratory. Typical examples of such direct methods are, for instance, Asch's (1956) 'confederate group' method or the methods employed in Lewin's (1935) studies of personality. The advantage of indirect methods is that they are less time consuming and more easy to apply compared to the direct methods; however, to be reliable they need an additional procedure of validization that is not necessary if direct methods are applied.

The studies presented in this book were mainly based on direct methods for two major reasons. First, the purpose of the studies was to trace the way children are (or can be) socialized, and not only taught, to become independent and moral individuals. Second, the studies also aimed to compare children's real behaviour with their verbal behaviour and for this their real behaviour had to be established in the first place.

As to the intervention stage, it is represented in developmental psychology to a lesser extent, partly because intervention has been traditionally viewed as a prerogative of practice and education, partly because of the technical difficulties that any intervention in a classroom or family involves. There are, however, some good examples of this type of study of motivation in children (see Lepper, 1983; Solomon *et al.*, 1988). This intervention stage of studies was of major interest for the studies presented in this book.

Conclusions

To review the studies presented, their main objectives may be formulated as follows:

1. To consider the development of early stages of personality as the unfolding of two mutually additive capacities: independence and morality.
2. To trace the development of independence and morality in the form of verbal behaviour and in the form of actual behaviour and to determine cognitive and motivational components of verbal and actual behaviours in children of various preschool ages and under varying experimental conditions.
3. To place emphasis on the exploration of the motivation of children's actual behaviour, with special reference to its analytic and intervention stages.

Note

1. The phenomenon of discrepancy between verbal and real behaviour does not pertain exclusively to the scope of individual psychology. It can also be observed on a mass scale in the behaviour of large groups of people. One of the most recent examples of such a discrepancy occurred during the general election campaign in the UK in 1992, when most of the public opinion polls almost unanimously predicted the Labour Party's victory. However, the Conservatives won.

Chapter 2

The formation of independent behaviour among preschoolers

An experimental analysis of conformity and independence

Preschoolers constantly observe other people's behaviour as they carry out daily activities. Even when there is no direct link between the child and the person being observed the other's actions substantially influence the child's behaviour; often the 'model's' actions are imitated (Bandura and Walters, 1964).

However, this imitation is most likely to appear if the model's actions do not contradict pre-existing patterns (or norms) that have been internalized by the child. Where there is contradiction, the child has to make a choice: whether to behave according to the old pattern and in opposition to the model, or to carry out the model's actions but violate the norm. Thus it is highly important to determine the child's ability to abstain from imitation; in other words, to be *independent* from the model.

It is necessary to distinguish between independence and autonomy. When children begin to eat, walk, dress themselves, and so forth their behaviour becomes autonomous – they need no help. Although in child psychology autonomy is sometimes interpreted as independence (see Amato and Ochiltree, 1986), in this book independence has a meaning similar to that used by Asch (1956). According to this usage, independence only appears in special critical situations involving a contrast between one's own actions or opinions with the actions or opinions of another.

It is also necessary to distinguish between independence and caprice. In an act of independence, a child contrasts a socially developed pattern he or she has assimilated earlier with another person's actions or behaviour, whereas in an act of caprice he or she expresses an individual whim. Thus, by independence I mean here *a child's behaviour that differs from the actions or opinions of another person when those actions or opinions do not accord with the child's prior experience or understanding of how to do this or that task.*

According to the definition, independence in its mature form involves a violation of standards, with the aim to install new and positive ways of thinking and behaviour. However, to be able to reveal independence like that an individual has to have an experience and a sophisticated intelligence that would allow him or her to make a subtle distinction between what is new and what is old, what is innovative and what is traditional, etc. In other words, in order to be able to overcome certain standard and traditional habits in thinking and behaviour the individual must be in command of those habits.

Of course, a young child can hardly be expected to have enough knowledge and sophistication to be independent in this mature form: obviously, the many layers of human life and experience (such as professional knowledge and habits, understanding of fine arts, subtle intuitions as to what is good and bad in human relations, etc.) are yet beyond the child's experience. Nevertheless, even a young child is already in command of certain (and rather numerous) programmes and rules of behaviour, which, being objective and conventional, may often be violated by other people.

Indeed, at school or in a family one can often observe the perplexity of a child who is witnessing unusual reactions of adults or older children in certain situations that are supposed to be well known and conventional for everybody, from unusual verbal behaviours (jokes, language accents, etc.) to deviant behaviours in social interactions. The particular case a child may be witnessing is the behaviour of a foreign person who inadvertently brings into social interactions in a new culture his or her original beliefs and attitudes. Another example is the behaviour of some teenagers in the street, which may well be in contradiction with what the young child was taught to be a good (or normal) way of behaviour. The young child is also not insured against witnessing some behaviours of close adults that may deviate from the conventional. All these situations are highly provocative with respect to the specific quality of the child's personality – his or her capacity to remain 'loyal' to previously assimilated beliefs and experiences, i.e. to reveal independence. Obviously, the same situations provide a measure for the child's conformity.

The situations mentioned above should not be mixed, however, with numerous situations in real life in which the child *reveals his or her caprices, whims and all sorts of naughty behaviour.* For example, the child may think that he or she does not need to go to bed when his or her mother does, or that he or she badly needs a particular toy from a superstore whereas the child's parents have a different opinion on the matter, etc. All these cases, however numerous and emotionally draining, have little to do with independence as it is interpreted in this book, since they are about conflicts between personal opinions and wishes and not between a stable and conventional programme, on the one hand, and deviations from it, on the other; the scale 'compliance vs. defiance' seems to be more appropriate for studying this type of conflict than the scale 'independence vs. conformity'.

It is also obvious from this definition that since independent behaviour rests upon a certain conventional programme it has a certain quality of 'rightness' that turns it into an adherence to a 'correct' and 'better' way of behaviour rather than merely adherence to an earlier learned habit. If habits can constitute a foundation for 'capricious' and 'naughty' behaviour, they cannot provide a basis for independent behaviour that refers exclusively to a certain stable, impersonal and context-independent programme.

In this respect independent behaviour can have a certain situational *moral value*, although it should not be identified with moral behaviour as such. Whereas moral behaviour is a subject's adherence to moral rules which are viewed as universal and obligatory for all people, independent behaviour is an adherence to *any type of stable programme* that may or may not relate to social context. The programmes that are used to measure independence may vary from universal rules (judgements about morality, for instance) to very situational and artificial ones (comparisons of lengths of lines, of certain visual patterns, of numbers of dots in visual arrays, etc.) and mostly do not bear the burden of 'moral necessity'. Apart from this basis, independent and moral behaviours also differ in their orientation. Independent behaviour is basically an individually oriented quality, it is a manifestation of the individual's capacity to be self-reliant in his or her judgements and actions regardless of other people's well-being; that is why independence, basically a positive personality feature, if unrestricted may sometimes grow into forms of behaviour that may cause damage to other people (see Chapter 1 above). In contrast, moral behaviour is oriented towards other people's well-being and, therefore, may sometimes run against the individual's personal interests and even impose restrictions on their independence. In sum, although independent and moral behaviours may share certain features and can sometimes intersect, they are different psychological qualities.

Another source of misunderstanding may originate from the interpretation of independence as autonomy. Basically, the development of autonomy in children is the development of competencies in various tasks, including manual tasks, intellectual tasks, language, self-control and self-regulation tasks, etc. (see, for instance, Blum and Blum, 1990; Crockenberg and Litman, 1990; Erikson, 1980). A general feature of this complex and multidimensional process is that the child is first taught or shown by peers and adults in what way he or she can cope with a certain task, and then gradually becomes able to do this task him/herself. In this process the child may proceed from initially coping with the task with the help of an adult (or a more competent peer) to the state when he or she is able to manage the task him/herself – the progress is best described by Vygotsky (1987) in his theory of the 'zone of proximal development'.

This liberation of the child from the necessity to be assisted in his or her activities is very often interpreted as the development of independence, and in a sense, it *is* independence – of a special kind. It is *independence from help, from assistance and from external control.* What is meant by independence in this book, however, is a different sort of independence. This is *independence from external influences able (and sometimes aimed) to diverge the child from the right way of behaviour, from the objective and conventional norms and programmes the child has already assimilated and interiorized.* If the first type of independence (i.e. autonomy) is independence from positive (helpful) social influences, the second type of independence is independence from negative (diverging, provocative) influences, which, directly or indirectly, deliberately or not, aim to bring a disorder into the child's experience and behaviour, into his or her convictions with regard to what people should and what they should not do in certain significant circumstances. This type of independence is already based on a certain degree of autonomy, on the child's knowledge of certain norms and programmes of behaviour. Traditionally, this second type of independence has been studied in the research of conformity.

The social value of the development of independent behaviour in the child is that it (1) helps to develop creative initiative and the ability to exceed the bounds of traditional tried-and-tested modes of behaviour and to give that 'creative extra' without which the development of the individual and of society is impossible, and (2) alters the way in which the child assimilates social experiences; from a general, imitative assimilation of all social influences, the child progresses to a selective assimilation of those influences that fit the social norms he or she has adopted, rejecting the situational influences from peers and adults that do not correspond to those norms.

The theoretical distinctions made above allow me not to consider here a vast range of studies concerned with the development of autonomy and self-regulation in children, which, being very interesting and important in themselves, seem to be irrelevant with regard to the notion of independence accepted in this book. Instead, a stress must be made upon the studies of conformative and nonconformative behaviour and their development in children.

While a good deal of attention has been paid to problems of social learning and the development of imitation, researchers have focused far less upon the development of nonconformity. Nevertheless, some important aspects of the problem have been investigated. In most of these studies, children have been asked to make judgements about some spatiotemporal or quantitative stimulus only after 'confederates' have expressed their opinions.

The goals of these studies were to measure the conformity or nonconformity of a child's behaviour as a factor of age, gender, task complexity, and so on. Thus Berenda (1950) stated that conformity was a negative function of age. However, contradictory results were obtained from research that showed an increase in conformity in children aged from 7 to 11 (Constanzo and Shaw, 1966; Iscoe, Williams and Harvey, 1963). In order to explain the discrepancies, Hamm and Hoving (1969) tried to define more precisely the investigative methods used in the earlier research. Following Deutsch and Gerard (1955), the authors divided conformity into 'normative' and 'informational' conformity. In the case of normative conformity, the subject accepts the confederate group's opinion because of his or her desire to be accepted socially, and despite the fact that 'in his or her mind' he or she disagrees with the group. In the case of informational conformity, the child agrees with the group's opinion because it seems to him or her to be correct.

According to Hamm and Hoving (1969) in some studies unambiguous tasks were used that tested normative conformity, while in other studies ambiguous tasks were used that thus allowed informational conformity. The authors then presented data which suggested that conforming behaviour was positively related to age if ambiguous tasks were employed and negatively related to age on unambiguous tasks. Later, reactions to ambiguous and unambiguous tasks were thoroughly studied in adult subjects (Penner and Davis, 1969; Campbell and Fairey, 1989). In another study, Hamm (1970) showed conformity to be a negative function of grade and a positive function of task ambiguity; he also found that nonconformity can be enhanced in children through the demonstration of models whose correct answers were reinforced, although the result was obtained for unambiguous tasks only.

Research into the influence of various confederate groups (peers, adults, parents, etc.) indicates that older schoolchildren are more prone to accept their peers' judgement than younger ones, whereas adult influence decreases (Aurora *et al.*, 1985; Hamm and Hoving, 1970; Utech and Hoving, 1969). However, contradictory results were obtained in research that varied the age and group size of confederates (Kumar, 1983). The roles of gender, race, socioeconomic status, self-categorization and personality have also been studied (Constanzo, 1970; Iscoe *et al.*, 1963, 1964; Vanderwiele and D'Hondt, 1983; Singh and Sharma, 1989; Abrams *et al.*, 1990).

Although both informative and helpful, these studies are limited in that they used children of advanced (mostly middle school) age, children's independence towards a group (rather than an individual) was tested, and verbal (rather than actual) behaviour was the focus. However, 'independence of judgement' does not guarantee that a child will be independent in deed as well as in word.

In order to overcome these limitations a new method of assessing children's independence has been proposed (Subbotsky, 1976). In the main bulk of the experiments three conflict situations (programmes) were used (see Figure 2.1). In the first situation, the child was given two objects (e.g. a little flag and a rattle); the experimenter had the same objects. The child was instructed to pick up the rattle when the experimenter picked up the flag, and vice versa. In the second

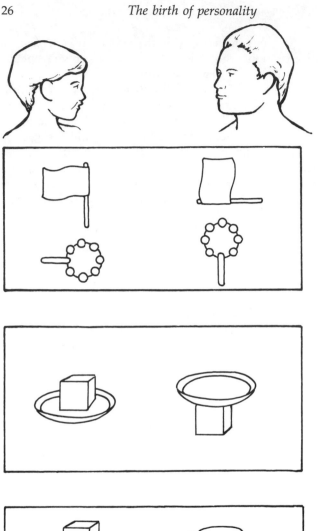

Figure 2.1 Basic programmes for 'independence' studies.

situation, a toy plate and a block were used. According to the instructions, after the experimenter had placed the block on the plate the child had to place the plate on the block, and so on. In the third situation, a toy cup was added to the plate and the block. The child was asked to place his or her block in the cup if the experimenter placed his or hers on the plate, and vice versa.

The experiment consisted of three conditions – a period of training and two subsequent experimental conditions. In the *training condition*, preschoolers were asked to carry out the tasks individually with the experimenter; the criterion for judging whether the child had mastered what was required was flawless execution of five actions in succession. The instruction was as follows: '[A name of the child], I'd like to play the game "a doll and a flag" with you. Look, I have a doll and a flag and you have a doll and a flag. Let's play like that: if I pick up my doll you should pick up your flag, and vice versa, if I pick up my flag you should pick up your doll, OK? Let's start now . . .' After the first task the next task followed, and so on. The training condition was followed by the *first experimental condition* (actual behaviour), in which the child was asked to participate with a confederate partner – who could either be a child from another preschool class or an adult. Each child usually performed twice, once with another child and once with an adult.

The experimental group included the child, his or her partner, and the experimenter (see Figure 2.2). The child and the partner sat facing each other at a table so that they could see each other's actions clearly; the experimenter sat to one side. All had the necessary sets of toys. The child and the partner took their cues from the experimenter's actions with the toys; their task was to carry out the conflict programmes they had learned in the training phase. If the partner was an adult person the experimenter gave the following instruction: '[A name of the child] and [a name of the adult partner] I'd like us to play together. Let's play the game 'a doll and a flag' exactly as I taught you earlier: if I pick up my doll both of you should pick up your flags, please, do it now . . . OK, and if I pick up my flag you should pick up your dolls, please, do it . . . OK [while the experimenter is giving the instruction the child and the partner are encouraged to accompany the experimenter's words with relevant actions]. Now I can see that you can do it all right. Let's start, then . . .'. The first experimental condition followed. During this condition, the partner first responded with two correct actions and then, unknown to the child, alternated

Figure 2.2 Independence: basic experimental situation.

randomly correct (conflicting with the experimenter's actions) and incorrect (imitating the experimenter) actions.

If a partner was another child the secret agreement to alternate right and wrong actions was not possible and the procedure was slightly different. The peer partner was first instructed (in the absence of a target child) to carry out the same programmes by just copying out the experimenter's actions. In the first experimental phase the instruction was as follows: 'Well, I'd like us to play the game "a doll and a flag" exactly as I taught you, OK? [a name of the target child], if I pick up this [the experimenter points out to his flag screening his toys from the peer partner with a small cardboard screen at the same time] what should you pick up? Do it, OK. And if I pick up this [the doll is pointed out] what should you pick up? Do this, OK. Now [a name of the peer partner] let's repeat the game with you [the same procedure follows]. Now I can see that both of you know how to play the game. Let's start then . . .' The first phase followed during which each child thought that the partner had been given the same instruction as him/herself.

Thus on occasion the children were in an indeterminate position, being forced either to do what their previous understanding of the task told them to do (and hence oppose their partner) or to follow their partner but violate the instructions. The experimenter performed 15 actions in succession; the children's actions and those of their partners were recorded. The task of the peer partner was an easier one than that of the target child (e.g. just to imitate the experimenter's actions). However, seeing the target child's actions the peer partner sometimes did the right actions, so that his or her behaviour resulted in the alternation of correct and incorrect actions.

In the *second experimental condition* (verbal behaviour), the experimenter removed the child's toys and asked him or her to indicate whether or not the partner had acted correctly; the partner's task was to behave as in the first condition, randomly alternating correct and incorrect (imitating the experimenter) actions. The instruction was as follows: 'Now I'd like to play only with [a partner's name] and you [a target child's name] just look and tell me whether [the partner's name] is doing right or wrong, OK?' After this each partner's response was followed by the experimenter's question to the target child 'And now what do you think, has [the partner's name] done right or wrong?' The goal was to determine to what extent children were capable of demonstrating independence at the verbal level.

This study was conducted in Moscow during 1970–6. Subjects were children of 2 years and 7 months to 6 years old. Subjects were drawn from kindergartens in Moscow serving a broad socioeconomic range.

This research (in part, it was published in my book, Subbotsky, 1976) showed that elements of independent behaviour take shape even in young preschoolers (3–4-year-olds).[1] They first appear when verbally assessing the actions of others and then, somewhat later, in the domain of actual deeds.

The comparison between the children's ability to verbally correct the partner's actions and their ability to show independent behaviour (e.g. not to follow the partner's wrong actions) in real actions with the same partner showed that the children could be allocated to the following groups. Children of the *first group* were not able either to verbally correct their partners (they acknowledged all the partner's actions to be correct) or to reveal independence relative to them (they copied out all the partner's wrong actions). Contrary to that, children of the *second group* could adequately verbally correct their partner's actions and showed complete independence in real actions.

Whereas in the children of the first and the second groups a certain uniformity between verbal and real behaviours was observed, children of the *third* and *fourth* groups revealed contradictory behaviours: either they could correctly verbally assess the partner's actions but failed to reveal independence in real actions (children of the third group) or they were unable to distinguish between the partner's right and wrong actions orally, but demonstrated complete independence in real actions (children of the fourth group). To determine the proportions in the overall sample of children two samples were taken: the first (217 children aged from 2 years 7 months to 6 years) contained children who had been checked on their ability to display independence (both in verbal and in actual behaviour) towards a peer partner, and the second (203 children of the same ages) contained children checked on their ability to be independent with an adult partner. Both samples of children were divided into four age categories: from 2 years 7 months to 3, from 3.1 to 4, from 4.1 to 5 and from 5.1 to 6. The ratios of children of the above mentioned groups among the samples of children of various ages are shown in Figure 2.3 (for a peer partner) and in Figure 2.4 (for an adult partner).

As the figures show, whereas the number of children who reveal independence only in their verbal behaviour is negligible, the number of children with the discrepancy of the opposite type is quite significant among younger children (2.7–4-year-olds) with respect to a peer partner, and in all the children (2.7–6 years) with regard to an adult partner. This means that there is a tendency for independent behaviour to appear first on the level of verbal judgements and only somewhat later on the level of real actions – *in the same child.*

The tendency for this independence to appear first in the children's verbal judgements and not in their real actions is also obvious if we compare the verbal performance of children (59 children aged 2.7 to 3, 62 children aged from 3.1 to 4, 35 children aged from 4.1 to 5 and 34 children aged from 5.1 to 6 – total 190) with an adult partner and the real performance of children (the numbers of children in each of the above mentioned age categories were 106, 90, 34 and 32 respectively – total 262) with an adult partner. Both samples were taken randomly from the kindergarten groups and consisted of

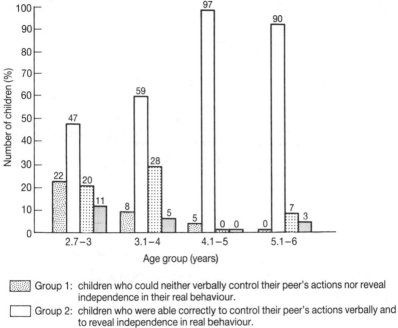

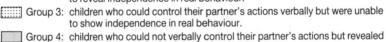

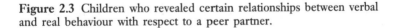

Group 1: children who could neither verbally control their peer's actions nor reveal independence in their real behaviour.

Group 2: children who were able correctly to control their peer's actions verbally and to reveal independence in real behaviour.

Group 3: children who could control their partner's actions verbally but were unable to show independence in real behaviour.

Group 4: children who could not verbally control their partner's actions but revealed independence in real behaviour.

Figure 2.3 Children who revealed certain relationships between verbal and real behaviour with respect to a peer partner.

children able to perform conflict programmes (see Figure 2.5). However, if we compare the verbal performance of children (the original sample consisted of 59 children aged from 2.7 to 3, 62 children aged 3.1 to 4, 35 children aged 4.1 to 5 and 35 children aged 5.1 to 6 – total 191 – taken randomly from various kindergarten groups and able to perform conflict programmes) with a peer partner and the real performance of same-age children (the original sample included 106 children aged 2.7 to 3, 90 children aged 3.1 to 4, 34 children aged 4.1 to 5, and 32 children aged 5.1 to 6, the total number 262, taken randomly from the kindergarten groups) with a

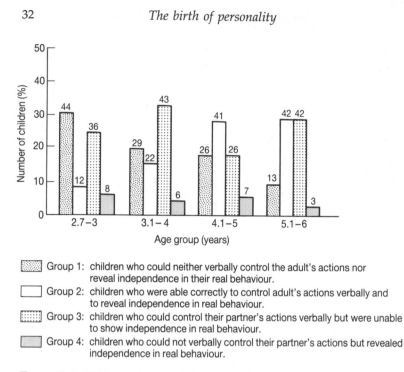

Figure 2.4 Children who revealed certain relationships between verbal and real behaviour with respect to an adult partner.

peer partner (see Figure 2.6), this comparison reveals the disparity only in children of a single age group (from 3.1 to 4).

In order to determine possible relationships between children's independence and the difficulties of the programme with regard to which independence (or lack of it) is revealed, I compared the children's verbal performance while making assessments of the partner's actions with regard to two types of programmes – conflict (described above) and nonconflict.

Two programmes were employed as nonconflict programmes. In the first (named 'toys'), the child (or the partner) was given a set of three different toys and asked to lift those among them that the experimenter named. During the execution the experimenter named the toys in a random order 10 to 15 times, and the child picked them up and put down accordingly. In the second programme (named 'house') the child was simply asked to built a house from blocks to

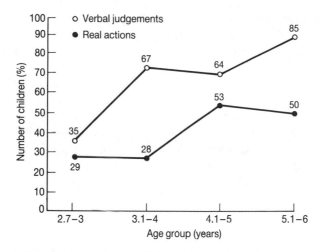

Figure 2.5 Children who revealed complete independence towards an adult partner.

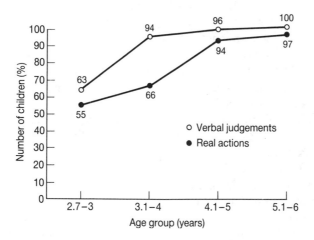

Figure 2.6 Children who revealed complete independence towards a peer partner.

reproduce a simple model previously built by the experimenter. It was assumed that the nonconflict programmes required less complex 'information processing' strategies from children than the conflict ones (for instance, they did not require a voluntary capacity to do the opposite to what the experimenter did). If the child's verbal independence is determined by the difficulties of the programme assessed, then the number of children who are able to reveal complete independence in their verbal judgements must be significantly larger among the children who assess the partner's actions according with the less complex (i.e. nonconflict) programmes than among children who assess the partner's execution of the more complex (i.e. conflict) programmes.

The original samples of children (all samples contained children of the same age categories: from 2 years 7 months to 3, from 3.1 to 4, from 4.1 to 5 and from 5.1 to 6) engaged in the assessment of the partners' (peers and adults) execution of the programmes (conflict and nonconflict) were as follows: 203 children (72 children, 64 children, 32 children, and 35 children in all the age categories, respectively) assessed actions of a peer partner and an adult partner performing nonconflict programmes; 190 children (59, 62, 35 and 34 children in all the age categories, respectively) assessed peers' and adults' performance of conflict programmes. Both samples were taken randomly from kindergarten groups. The results (Figure 2.7) revealed no significant differences between the numbers of children showing complete verbal independence towards partners carrying out conflict and nonconflict programmes. No significant differences were found when the children who managed to assess well their peers' actions with respect to both conflict (numbers of subjects in the above mentioned age groups were 31, 40, 35 and 34 respectively – total 140) and nonconflict (numbers of subjects 27, 42, 30, and 34 respectively – total 133) programmes were asked to control verbally adult partners' actions with regard to the same programmes (Figure 2.8). The findings showed that the difficulty of the programme itself (conflict vs. nonconflict) did not significantly influence the children's verbal capacity to reveal independent (or conformative) behaviour. The same tendency that was observed on the basis of conflict programmes (the larger number of children were able to reveal complete independence towards their peers than towards adults) was also present in the findings based on nonconflict programmes (see Figure 2.7), although

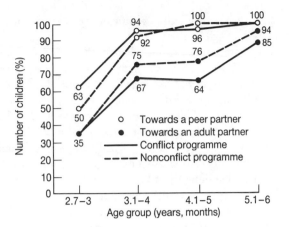

Figure 2.7 Children who revealed verbal independence towards their partners with regard to the partner's fulfilment of conflict and nonconflict programmes.

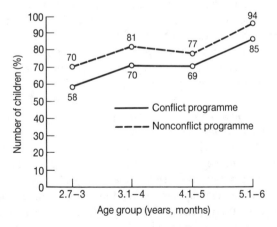

Figure 2.8 Children who revealed independence towards an adult in their verbal judgements with regard to the adult's fulfilment of conflict and nonconflict programmes among children who earlier revealed verbal independence towards their peers.

The birth of personality

the differences were statistically significant ($p < 0.05$) in one age group only (4.1- to 5-year-olds).

In sum, the data show quite clearly that *the development of independence in children's real actions lags behind the development of the same quality in children's verbal judgements*. The question arises about the causes of this lag. One might assume that *independence in real actions requires more matured intellectual functions and voluntary behaviour from the child than does independence in verbal judgements*. If this is the case then children who were able verbally to correct their adult partner's actions but failed to show independent behaviour relative to the adult in their real actions, should not be able to act independently relative to a peer partner as well, since independence in real actions requires the same intellectual functions and voluntary behaviour irrespective of the partner with whom the child is doing the programme.

In order to check this I asked the children from the above mentioned group (Group 3 in Figure 2.4) to fulfil the same programmes with a peer partner. As a result, 70 per cent of the children from all the age groups showed complete independence towards a peer. This makes the hypothesis of the 'intellectualistic' origins of the lag between children's independence in their real and verbal behaviours unlikely.

Another possible explanation of the lag stems from the fact that it was mainly observed in children when they were carrying out programmes with an adult partner (Figure 2.5), and it was significantly less salient with respect to a peer partner (Figure 2.6). Since the only difference between an adult and a peer partner doing the same actions for the child may have been in the child's emotional attitude towards them, I assumed that *it was just this attitude that made real independent action with respect to an adult (e.g. to an authoritative person) more difficult than the verbal correction*.

Indeed, it is normally easier to criticize the actions of an authoritative person verbally than to act contrary to that person, because a verbal action is a reversible one and may be excused, whereas a real action usually has irreversible consequences. But if this hypothesis is true, then *it must be more difficult for the children to exercise independence towards adults than towards peers both in real actions and in verbal judgements, since it must be less probable for them to experience a wrong action by the adult partner than by a peer partner*. To examine this I asked children (the age categories included 59 children aged 2 years

7 months to 3, 62 children aged 3.1 to 4, 35 children aged 4.1 to 5 and 34 children aged 5.1 to 6 – total 190) taken randomly from the kindergarten groups and able to perform conflict programmes first to correct peers' actions and then to correct adults' actions. The results (Figure 2.9) confirmed the expectation. In each age category there was a significant proportion of children who could control the peer's actions well but acknowledged all the adult's actions to be correct; however, there were no subjects who could verbally correct the adult's actions but did not notice the errors in the peer.

The same discrepancy was recorded when children's actions relative to adults were compared to their actions relative to a peer partner (the age samples consisted of 106 children aged 2 years 7 months to 3, 90 subjects aged 3.1 to 4, 34 subjects aged 4.1 to 5 and 32 subjects aged 5.1 to 6 – total 262 – taken randomly from kindergarten groups and able to perform conflict programmes): a significantly larger number of children could act independently with respect to a peer than with respect to an adult (Figure 2.10).

The data show that even if all the necessary intellectual skills (that is, an ability to compare the partner's actions with the programme, to use the appropriate verbal terms, etc.) and the necessary level of voluntary behaviour (a capacity to overcome the tendency to imitate

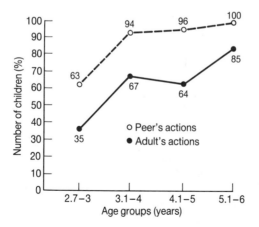

Figure 2.9 Children who could successfully correct their peer's actions and adult's actions.

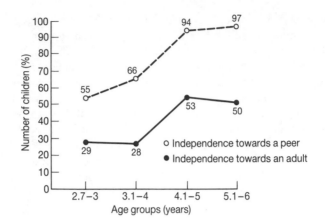

Figure 2.10 Children who showed independence towards a peer and an adult in their real actions.

blindly what the experimenter or the partner is doing) are available, the child still has to overcome something in order to be able to act independently from the adult partner. It seemed reasonable to assume that *this 'something' is only the child's emotional attitude towards an adult as to an 'infallible' model.*

Indeed, the social position a young child occupies in a society is such that the child is normally expected to learn from adults, to imitate them, whereas an adult is supposed to teach and to control the child's actions. Since a preschool child has to conform systematically to these expectations they can well create in the child a certain emotional image of an adult as an 'infallible model' whom he or she is expected to imitate. It is just this emotional global imitative attitude (GIA) that may have forced children to imitate the adult's wrong actions despite the fact that the children had shown complete independence with respect to their peers.

However, this hypothesis has an alternative. Indeed, the child may acknowledge all the wrong actions by the adult partner to be correct (verbal conformity) or imitate them in his or her real actions not because he or she thinks they are correct (it would be logical to expect this based on the GIA hypothesis) but simply because the child does not have the courage to say overtly (by a word or an action) that they are incorrect. An alternative hypothesis, therefore, is that *the imitative behaviour could have been a result of the are children's fear that their independent actions would not be welcomed by an adult.* Specifically, the children could declare that all the partner's actions were correct (verbal behaviour), or copy the partner's actions (actual behaviour), even though the children believed them to be incorrect, simply for fear of disapproval – in spite of the fact that, under experimental conditions, both the experimenter and the children's partner were supposed not to express any reaction towards the children's actions, whether correct or incorrect.

This hypothesis is supported by the fact that first, overt non-conformity of a preschool child to an adult is not typically approved of in the cultural region from which these subjects were drawn. Second, in this experimental situation one cannot discount the possibility that there could be some involuntary facial or gestural response to the children's actions. Third, it is possible that the children could imagine and anticipate disapproval; this 'imaginary control' could, of course, exert a large influence on the children's behaviour.

In order to test this hypothesis that the findings were partly caused by the partner's direct or indirect influence over the child, the first 'screening' experiment was conducted (Subbotsky, 1983b). In this experiment subjects (70 children of 3, 4, 5 and 6 years participated, in numbers 25, 14, 18 and 13 respectively, taken randomly from various kindergartens in Moscow) were tested individually, in two conditions. In the first condition (no screening), the procedure was identical to that described above in this chapter. It was aimed to determine the children's independence in the domain of verbal assessments and actual behaviour with an adult confederate partner. In the second condition (screening), all but the partner's hands was invisible behind a screen, so that the children could observe what the partner did but remain unobserved themselves (see Figure 2.11). Otherwise the procedure was identical to that used in the first condition, with the exception that when the children were asked to respond verbally they were asked to whisper to the experimenter.

The hypothesis was that *under the screening condition, the children's fear of the partner's disapproval would be substantially weakened or disappear.* Thus if fear determined the incorrect imitation in the nonscreening condition, under the screening condition the children's behaviour should exhibit more independence.

A conformity score (K) was calculated, based on the results of each child's behaviour. When the children were asked to respond verbally, K equalled the ratio of the number of the partner's incorrect actions

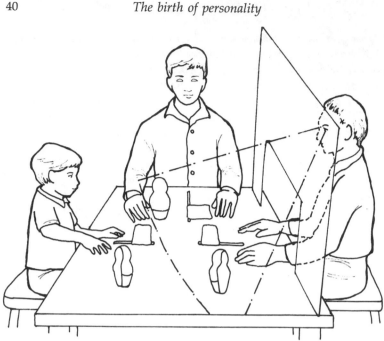

Figure 2.11 The 'screening' experiment.

that the child assessed as being correct to the number of the partner's incorrect actions. When the child was actually required to carry out the actions, K equalled the ratio of imitation of incorrect partner's actions to the number of incorrect partner's actions. K was assessed for each of the three different sets of stimulus materials and then averaged for each of the two types of response (verbal and actual behaviour) and for each of the experimental conditions (screening and no screening).

The comparisons between conditions and between response type showed that there was no main effect for screening (see Figure 2.12) either in verbal response or behavioural response. These findings, therefore, did not support the hypothesis that the children's imitation of their partner's incorrect actions resulted from fear of disapproval, for in every age group the screening procedure did not lead to a decrease in conformity. Instead, the results support the original hypothesis that children's conformity may be a result of their belief in the adult partner's 'infallibility'.

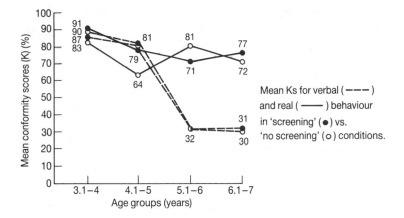

Figure 2.12 The 'screening the partner' experiment.

The goal of the second experiment was to analyze the motivation for independent behaviour. As was the case with conformity, in this type of experimental situation independent behaviour may be based on at least two motivating factors. One such factor could be external control (children's drive to get the experimenter's approval for not copying their partner's actions or, their fear of disapproval). While under the experimental conditions the experimenter abstained from overt assessment of the children's actions, he could nevertheless influence the children's behaviour through 'reflective anticipation'. In this case, the experimenter's assessment exists only in the imagination of the child – yet nevertheless it may prove a powerful influence. Obviously, this type of independent behaviour (I call it 'pragmatic independence') is motivated by extrinsic forces and can be called 'independence' only symbolically since the child's independence from a partner turns out here to be his or her dependence from the experimenter's control. This externally motivated nonconformity (independence) does exist, and can be enhanced through vicarious reinforcement (observation of the model whose correct actions were rewarded), as it was shown in empirical studies (Hamm, 1970).

On the other hand, the motivation of independent behaviour may stem from the children's desire simply to do the programme well, i.e. from their awareness of the 'rightness' of performing this programme in this way and not in a different way. Indeed, in so far as the children carried out the actions appropriately in the training sessions, inappropriate actions (occasioned by the partner's incorrect actions) were unlikely to be perceived as simple mistakes or slips, but rather acquired a status of 'transgressions'. Thus a second motivating factor in independent behaviour could be the children's desire to keep the 'indirect promise' that they make to the experimenter to carry out the conflict programme correctly even if the partner carried it out incorrectly. This type of motivation is of intrinsic rather than of extrinsic origin; it belongs rather to the realm of morality and self-esteem and is not a matter of mere obedience.

To answer this question, it was necessary to prevent any possibility of the children feeling any indirect sense of control, which was the goal of Experiment 2. Subjects consisted of 56 children divided into three age groups (21 3–4-year-olds; 18 5-year-olds; 17 6-year-olds) all of whom were from the same preschool.

The procedure was similar to that used in Experiment 1; the difference was that the experimenter (and not an adult partner) was screened under the second experimental condition. In this condition the screen was placed so that the children could only see the experimenter's hands. During 'verbal' assessment under this screening condition, the child was instructed to answer the experimenter's questions nonverbally, by nods or shakes of the head. Thus from the children's point of view, their opinions remained unknown to the experimenter. Responses were anonymously recorded by an assistant.

All the children who took part in this experiment revealed considerable independence ($K < 0.5$) under the first experimental condition (no screening). Our hypothesis was that *screening would be perceived by the child as eliminating any possibility for experimenter's control. If independent behaviour under the first experimental condition was determined by the 'imaginary control', then under the screening condition it should decrease considerably*. As a result, no 'screening effect' was found for any of the age groups in either the verbal or the actual sphere of behaviour (see Figure 2.13).

These results supported the hypothesis that motivation of independent behaviour revealed in the basic experimental testing situation was of intrinsic rather than of extrinsic nature. The absence of any 'screening effect' indicated that children's independent actions in the standard experimental situation were caused rather by their desire to do what they had agreed to do and thought a right thing to do than by a tendency to win the experimenter's approval, whether real or

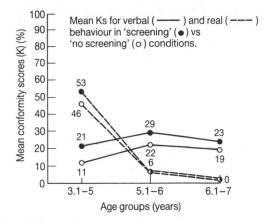

Figure 2.13 The 'screening the experimenter' experiment.

imaginary. It is this type of independence (it may be called 'unpragmatic independence' in contrast to the externally controlled 'pragmatic independence') that we are going to consider in further research. The analysis and the development of 'pragmatic independence' that can be achieved through various types of reinforcement (either positive or negative) is, of course, a special task which, however, remained beyond the studies reviewed in this chapter.[2]

In general, the data showed that the development of independent behaviour in preschool-age children is a combined result of complex cognitive and motivational changes. The next stage of the study was, therefore, to determine what kinds of changes are necessary and sufficient conditions for independent behaviour to arise. With this stage we pass from the analysis of the psychological structure of conformative and independent behaviour in children to the intervention stage.

Enhancing independent behaviour in preschoolers: intervention studies

As was mentioned above, there might be at least two main causes that can shift a preschool child from a global-imitative behaviour to an independent one, provided, of course, that a necessary level of voluntary behaviour is achieved. First, it may be assumed that the leading role in this transition belongs to the development of cognitive functions, namely (1) to *the development of the children's competence in mastering various sorts of programmes* (such as language, actions with human artifacts, social interactions, etc.) and (2) to *the development of an awareness that other people (in particular adults) can sometimes carry out the programmes in a wrong way.*

It is quite obvious that both of these capacities may be the necessary conditions for independence to emerge: one can hardly expect a person to be able to reveal independence in a certain action (for instance, in speaking native language) if that person is not an expert in doing this kind of action (for example, cannot speak his or her native language well enough). However, even if expert the person can be unaware that another person is doing something wrongly (for instance, speaking badly) and, therefore, can follow the other person's mistakes simply because he or she adopts the other person's behaviour as a more correct one.

Nevertheless, even if both of the distinguished intellectual capacities are available, the child still may imitate another person's mistakes because it regards that person as an authority. In this case the cause for global imitation does not lie in the child's lack of certain intellectual prerequisites, but in its GIA towards the person. To overcome conformity in this case *the child's GIA towards a partner should be eliminated.*

In order to compare the role of the three selected factors (mastering the programmes, acquisition of awareness of the partner's mistakes and elimination of GIA), the intervention experiment was conducted (Subbotsky, 1976). Fifty-one children (age range 2 years 7 months to 3 years 11 months) participated as subjects. Since in the pretests all the children showed their capacity correctly to perform the conflict programmes with a peer partner, it went without saying that they had reached the necessary level of voluntary behaviour maturity.[3] However, the children failed to show independence towards an adult partner both in their verbal judgements and in their real actions.

According to the first and the second hypotheses, to foster independent behaviour in the children towards an adult partner one should either train the children to fulfil the programmes (in order to make the programmes more salient) or help them to become aware of the fact that the adult partner sometimes makes mistakes. Sixteen and fifteen children respectively were allocated to the first and second experimental conditions. In the first condition the children were trained to perform the programmes tête-à-tête with the experimenter; in the second they were taught to correct the actions of the adult partner verbally. Both methods proved to be ineffective: in control experiments the great majority of the children failed to demonstrate independence. Despite the fact that they were taught to perform the programmes almost automatically and corrected their partner's actions perfectly, 70–80 per cent of them continued to imitate all the wrong actions of the adult partner.

If the third hypothesis is correct, then it was the emotional attitude towards an adult and not the lack of any intellectual skills that caused the conformative behaviour. Since this attitude may have been a consequence of the children's specific social position in society (the position of a subordinated person who must learn and imitate adults' actions but cannot teach and control the adults) it is just the change in the position that could destroy GIA in children and result in more independent behaviour subsequently; therefore, it was necessary to put the child in the position of a leader who can teach the adult and exert control over his or her actions.

This was done in the third experimental condition (with 20 subjects). The experimenter told the child that the adult partner 'didn't know' the programmes and the child had to teach him or her. Usually the child was very pleased and proud of his or her new leading role and agreed enthusiastically. When the 'teaching' was finished, the control experiment was carried out in which the child and the adult participated again as equal partners. Now almost all the children revealed complete independence.

This shows that neither the children's own competence in performing the programmes nor their knowledge that the adult is incompetent are sufficient for the children to become independent. What the child needs is to feel that he or she is a leader, 'a teacher and controller' of the adult's actions. This feeling can be created through the change in the child's social position. As the study showed, this change was enough to destroy the child's GIA and to foster his or her independence provided that all the necessary intellectual skills were available.

The role of the style of social interaction in the development of conformative and independent behaviour

The results of the intervention experiment prompted me to look more closely at the nature of what had happened in the third experimental condition. It was obvious that the only difference between this condition and the second was that in the third condition the child was not merely shown that the adult partner could perform wrong actions. In this condition the child was also *treated as an equal and even superior to the adult partner.*

In order to stress this feature of a social interaction between a child and an adult – equality or inequality of the partnership – I applied the term 'style of social interaction'. Among many possible variations two styles seem to be particularly relevant to the development of independent and conformative behaviour. In an *authoritarian style* of social interaction (ASI) one party has the opportunity of controlling, and in fact does control, the actions of another in his or her interests; the other party does not have this possibility. In a *democratic style* of social interaction (DSI), both parties have equal rights to control, and indeed do control, each other's actions according to certain common rules or programmes.

It has been assumed that what was called independent and conformative behaviours in children are, in fact, consequences of the prevalent styles of social interactions. More precisely, *the conformative behaviour (and the GIA towards adults) is a result of a prevalence of the authoritarian style in social interactions between preschool children and adults. As the democratic style of social interactions gradually replaces ASI the independence in the children's behaviour arises.*

Studies of social interaction styles in terms of 'parenting styles' have a rather long tradition in psychology. Sears *et al.* (1957) were, perhaps, among the first who attracted scholars' attention to the role childrearing practices (i.e. restrictiveness and permissiveness) play in the development of children's personalities. Baumrind (1971), in a series of studies based upon interview and real-life observations, distinguished authoritarian, authoritative and permissive parenting styles and studied the effects the styles had on the development of various personality characteristics in children. She found that children of authoritarian parents revealed low social competence in their interactions with peers, low initiative in social contacts and a tendency to rely upon outside authority in moral conflict situations. If authoritarian parenting has a discouraging effect on autonomy in children, authoritative parenting encourages autonomy and social competence: authoritative parents are basically warm and nurturant towards children while placing certain limits on their initiatives at the same time. Children of authoritative parents are more socially competent, more self-reliant than the children of authoritarian parents. Permissive parents tend to abstain, although for various reasons, from overt control over their children's behaviour. Contrary to popular expectations, their children are relatively incompetent and immature in their social interactions and experience difficulties in controlling their impulsive tendencies.

In more recent classifications a distinction has been made between neglectful (indifferent) and permissive–indulgent types of parenting (Maccoby and Martin, 1983). The first type is characterized by parents' noninvolvement in their children's lives and by parents' indifference to their children's interests. Permissive–indulgent parents are, on the contrary, involved in their children's lives and activities but place few demands and controls on them since many of them believe this may enhance confidence and creativity in children. However, both types of parenting have many similar consequences in that the children of such parents often reveal relatively little social competence and lack of self-control, they may be capricious and self-centred. Cross-cultural variations in parenting styles were also found (Whiting and Edwards, 1988).

The studies of parenting styles, although extensive, mainly focused on the development of children's autonomy (social competency, self-reliance and self-control) and certain other characteristics (such as maturity of moral judgements – see Chapter 3 for a review). There is no direct evidence available that one of the parenting styles (for instance, authoritarian) enhances conformative behaviour in children, and that the other one (for example, authoritative) facilitates independence. Nevertheless, some of the classifications of parenting styles (for instance, Baumrind's authoritarian vs. authoritative) come very close to the scale 'authoritarian vs. democratic' styles of social interaction accepted in the present book.

The studies also provide indirect evidence in favour of our hypothesis. Thus, the fact that children of restrictive and authoritarian parents are more inclined to rely upon external authority in their moral judgements than children of responsive but demanding parents (Dunton, 1989; Hart, 1988) may be interpreted as encouraging for the hypothesis of the positive relationships between children's independence and their experience of the democratic style of the social interaction, on the one hand, and between children's conformity and the authoritarian style of social interaction, on the other. However, indirect evidence should be treated with caution, and a special study on the above mentioned relationships is necessary.

To examine the hypothesis, the impact that various styles of social interaction may have on children's behaviour was subjected to a special examination (Subbotsky and Drobotova, 1980). In Experiment 1 the children who participated had shown complete independence in their real behaviour (with $K = 0$) towards adult partners in the normal testing procedures in which three conflict programmes (described above) were involved (pretest phase). A child and an adult partner were presented with the new and more complex programme (training phase). The child was told that 'now we are going to play as before'; however, the experimenter offered the child and his/her adult partner a new, unknown programme. Each of the participants were given three identical objects; a cup, a plate and a spoon. According to the programme, the child and the adult had to put their spoons in their cups and their cups on their plates each time the experimenter put his/her spoon on his/her plate leaving his/her cup in its original place. If the experimenter put his/her cup on his/her plate leaving his/her spoon in its place, the partners had to put their spoons in their cups and leave their plates in their places; if the experimenter put his/her cup and his/her spoon on his/her plate, the partners had to put their plates on their cups and leave their spoons in their places. After a brief introduction the adult partner (who had been taught the programme earlier) did the programme well whereas the child, of course, did not. After a few minutes the experimenter asked the adult to teach the child to do the programme. While teaching, the adult partner exercised the authoritarian style of social interaction: he or she corrected the child's errors with a firm voice, reproaching him or her for mistakes and wearing a 'commanding' facial expression. After the child had learnt the programme, he or she was again subjected to the series of posttests (posttest phase). In this series the three standard conflict programmes (Condition 2) or the new programme (Condition 1) were employed with the same adult partner who taught the child in the training phase. In Condition 3 of the posttest the child performed a new programme with a new adult partner. During this procedure a programme (those employed in the 'teaching phase' vs. the programme employed in the pretest) and a partner (the partner who taught the child vs. a new adult partner) were varied.

The children in the control group were not subjected to authoritarian teaching, instead they were taught the new programme by the experimenter in the presence of the adult partner. In the pretest phase 122 children aged from 3 to 7 took part. For the training phase 80 of them who showed complete independence were selected; they were recruited in the experimental and control groups (40 subjects in each, divided into age samples of 3 to 3 years 11 months, 4 to 4.11, 5 to 5.11 and 6 to 7, with each age sample containing 10 children).

As expected, in the posttest the children of the experimental group revealed much stronger conformity towards the authoritarian adult partner than did the children of the control group when the new programme (but not the original programme used in the pretest) was employed (see Table 2.1, Conditions 1 and 2). They also conformed towards the new adult partner to the same extent as they did towards the authoritarian adult partner (Table 2.1, Condition 3).

The experiment thus showed that the authoritarian style of social interaction does foster conformative behaviour in children. However, this influence is only evident with respect to the new programme and not to the programme in which the children had already shown their independence towards the adult partner in the pretest. But will this independence continue if the authoritarian communication lasts longer and is more comprehensive than that used in Experiment 1?

Table 2.1 Mean conformity scores (K,%) of children's real behaviour in experimental and control groups in Conditions 1–3

| Age samples (years, months) | Condition | | | | | | |
| | 1 | | | | 2 | | 3 |
	Exper. group	Contr. group	t	Level of signific.	Exper. group	Contr. group	Exper. group
3–3.11	100	20	12	.001	0	0	80
4–4.11	100	12	14.4	.001	0	0	80
5–5.11	90	5	7.2	.001	0	0	100
6–7	70	2	4.2	.01	0	0	70

The birth of personality

To address this question Experiment 2 was conducted. In this experiment a group of children was subjected to either authoritarian (adult A) or democratic (adult D) styles of social interaction. In the pretests children's initial Ks (verbal and real behaviours with respect to an adult partner) were determined according to the standard procedure employing three original conflict programmes. After that two adults (who did not participate in the pretests) systematically communicated with the children during a month (a training phase). The adults (two female university students) visited the children at different times and suggested that they should 'study together' certain subjects (language, modelling, drawing). During the studies adult A practised an authoritarian style (in the same way as in Experiment 1), whereas adult D practised a 'mild' democratic style: she asked the children to show her what adult A had taught them and then to teach her the same. During the communication she behaved in a democratic way, always had a positive and warm facial expression and often asked the children to control and correct her actions. In posttests the children had adults A (Condition 1) and B (Condition 2) as their partners. The same three standard programmes as in the pretest were employed.

Twenty-eight children participated as subjects: 10 in the younger age sample (from 3 to 4) and 18 in the older age sample (from 4 to 6). The results showed that the independence in children's real actions in the posttest was significantly lower towards adult A and significantly higher towards adult D than it was in the pretest (see Table 2.2). The results, therefore, favour the hypothesis that ASI prompts the

Table 2.2 Mean conformity scores (K,%) of children's real (K_r) and verbal (K_v) behaviour in Conditions 1 and 2

Age samples (years)	K	Condition 1				Condition 2			
		Pre-test	Post-test	t	Level of signif.	Pre-test	Post-test	t	Level of signif.
3–4	K_r	37	64.5	−3.4	0.01	37	7.5	2.3	0.05
	K_v	26	51	−1.9	ns	26	4	2.4	0.05
5–6	K_r	19.7	35.8	−2.7	0.05	19.7	10.3	2.5	0.02
	K_v	8.3	22.2	−2.14	0.02	8.3	2.5	1.3	ns

development of conformative behaviour in children, whereas DSI facilitates independent behaviour. However, both studies were arranged as laboratory experiments. To determine whether DSI, if it is systematically applied in classroom work, enhances the development of independent behaviour, Experiment 3 was conducted.

The idea of this experiment (Subbotsky, 1981a) was based on our observation that the prevalent traditional style of social interaction between teachers and children in Moscow kindergartens was mainly an authoritarian one. According to this prevailing style the most valuable quality of the preschool children's personality is viewed in the children's general imitativeness and their belief in adult's infallibility. The image of the adult that is created and maintained in this style of education is that of an ideal bearer of social experience, a model for global emulation. The other side of the image that is a natural part of any real human being – his or her vacillations, doubts and mistakes – is carefully concealed from the child.

The inculcation of a democratic style of social interaction[4] requires a break with traditional authoritarian relations between children and the educator, i.e. relations that normatively assign the function of model and controller to the adult and the function of imitating subject to the child. This break involves two essential changes: (1) an equalization of the demands made on the respective behaviours of adult and child by which both children and educator may equally exercise the functions of model and controller, and (2) the educator's repudiation of social control over the child's acts (rewards and punishments) as much as possible. As a result, the images that adults and children have of one another lose their abstract and one-sided character and become, in a sense, more 'stereoscopic': on the one hand, the child is looked at as a person who, although being very 'imperfect' and 'insufficient' in many of his or her capacities, nevertheless has something that he or she can offer and teach an adult (as this actually is in reality); on the other hand, an adult loses part of his/her 'perfectness' and turns to the child with his/her 'vulnerable' side, that is, reveals that he/she can sometimes be wrong, can experience vacillations and doubts and that his/her difference from a child is not as absolute and unquestionable as it was portrayed within the authoritarian style of social interaction. In other words, within the democratic style of social interaction children can enjoy the image of an adult in which both 'official' and 'unofficial' parts of the whole image are combined at one time.

Another characteristic feature of the democratic style is the active role of the adult. Within the authoritarian style of interaction the adult's role is 'responsive', in the sense that the teacher has to wait until children do something with respect to what he/she suggests and then to react (i.e. to reward some types of children's behaviour and to punish others). In contrast, within the democratic style this is a teacher who initiates the communication: before he/she can expect to get something from children (for instance, their respect, love or their desire to do what he/she asks them to) the adult first has to offer the children something that they value (an upgrading in their social position, an interesting game, an amusing conversation, etc.). Consequently, if the authoritarian style of social interaction can easily be conceived in terms of 'conditioning', the democratic style looks more like a sort of 'investment' (if such a term is appropriate in human relations) – an 'investment' whose 'profits' can be expected to materialize, but in a substantial period of time.

Accordingly, we constructed tasks in two kindergarten classes in which the educator and the children alternately occupied the position of 'pupil' and 'teacher'. A group of children and two adults, an educator and an assistant, participated in the lessons. In the first part of the lesson, the children had to learn programme material under the guidance of the educator. The assistant, who sat at the table with the children, did the same things they did; his or her behaviour was not supposed to differ from theirs. In the second part, the educator asked one of the children to reproduce the material he or she had learned in the first part, and the other children to check his or her actions. In the third part of the exercise, the educator asked the assistant to reproduce the same material, and the children then had to check his or her actions and show the adult the correct models of behaviour. During the course of this reproduction, the assistant would alternate correct actions with incorrect actions in random order, and the children would check and correct him or her.

Neither the educator nor the assistant was allowed to use authoritarian measures (raise the voice, rebuke, punish). The educator was permitted to use mild forms of social control (requests, remonstrations), but the behaviour of the assistant had to be even and gentle (sometimes displaying a slight lack of confidence), and have his/her facial expression positive and tone of voice happy; he or she could not respond with sanctions to any of the children's actions with respect to him or her, even those that contained elements of aggression and negativity (of course, within reasonable limits, i.e. as long as the child's actions did not threaten the dignity and well-being of the other children and the experimenter).

It was assumed that in arranging interaction between the children and the educators in this way we would approximate the democratic style of social interaction. During this interaction not one, but two adults performed the role of educator, each of whom embodied one of the aspects of the adult: that of an 'ideal model for emulation' and that of 'doubts, vacillations and mistakes'. To prevent any rigid attachment to either of these two aspects in one specific adult, the educator and the assistant changed roles each week. The second necessary condition for such communication was that the discussion between child and adult should ultimately lead to discovery of the truth.

Thus, two goals were achieved at the same time: the transmission of experience from adult to child was ensured, and both criteria of DSI were met (equal demands made of both child and adult and repudiation of social control over the child's actions).

The pre- and posttests were administered to each child in the experimental and control groups (in which the traditional authoritarian style of social interaction was preserved) before and after the educational-formative experiment. The three conflict programmes described above were used. The coefficient of emulation (conformity score – K) was calculated as described above. Hence, the behaviour of each child was characterized by four average coefficients in 12 test situations, as shown in Table 2.3.

A comparison of these coefficients in the pre- and posttests should show any change in the children's inclination towards independent behaviour to be a result of formative efforts (experimental groups) or

Table 2.3 Conformity scores (K) used in the pretests and posttests

Partner	Type of Behaviour	
	Real	Verbal
Peer($_p$)	K_{rp}	K_{vp}
Adult ($_a$)	K_{ra}	K_{va}

any such change that had taken place in the course of lessons using the usual procedure (control groups).

For a quantitative comparison of the spontaneous creative activity of the children in the experimental and control groups in clay modelling and drawing exercises, parallel test exercises were carried out in the last stage of the programme. Both groups of children were given identical models and assignments. The results of their activity were compared in terms of two parameters reflecting creative activity: the number of elements done in excess of the assignment (which included doing the assignment the second time, new elements introduced by the child into the assignment, new drawings and figures) and the number of elements not contained in the model (only the number of new drawings and figures not resembling the model and the number of new elements introduced by the child into the assignment were calculated; identical elements were counted as one).

In the formative experiments, junior (3–4-year-olds) and middle (4–5-year-olds) groups at nursery kindergarten no. 676 of the Gagarin district of Moscow participated. Similar groups from another kindergarten in Moscow participated in the control groups. Educators of the experimental groups (four persons) and a group of psychologists participated in the experimental programme. The exercises were conducted daily (with the exception of Sundays and holidays) with a two-week break in early January. The type and number of exercises are indicated in Table 2.4.

Table 2.4 Types of experimental lessons

Type of lesson	Number of lessons	
	Younger group	Middle group
Drawing and modelling	13	16
Modelling	20	18
Native language	26	23
Mathematics	14	12
Physical education	23	21
Designing	8	3
Appliqué work	2	3
Total	106	96

All the exercises contained extensive and varied material. Thus, lessons in the native language included looking at slides, reading stories, learning verses and funny stories by heart, serious reading and educational games; lessons in physical education included learning various movements, free exercises, sports, etc. The same lessons, with slight variations, were carried out by the control groups using the traditional procedure. The pre- and posttests were carried out in October and April 1980.

A number of stages were clearly evident in the *overall course of the educational-formative experiment*. In the first stage, the children were typically perplexed and puzzled by what was taking place. Verbal checking of the actions of an adult predominated. Many children pointed out the incorrectness of the actions of the assistants, but were too shy to demonstrate the correct model. In the second stage, the assistant's wrong actions began to arouse friendly laughter. The children watched his or her behaviour with constant interest, commenting on the slightest mistake, often called even correct adult's actions incorrect (hypercriticism), and began to rebuke the adult outside the experimental situation ('But you didn't close the door', 'You weren't sitting on the chair properly', etc.). During the course of the exercises, discussions would spontaneously arise among the children on whether the adult had done something correctly or incorrectly; this discussion would involve the entire group. In the third stage, some of the children began to correct the actions of their peers and the adults spontaneously, without any prompting from the educator. The children were happy when the assistant performed the action correctly; some even cried aloud with glee and applauded. But in addition to making proper corrections and displaying acts of independence, many of the children were imitative, and were uncritical towards the actions of their peers and adults; imitative actions were also encounted in the most active children. It is interesting that the intensity and the quality of spontaneous corrections depended on the difficulty of the material learned. When easy tasks were to be performed, the children actively corrected one another and the assistant, but complicated assignments caused them to concentrate their attention on actual performance technique, and reciprocal monitoring was reduced to a minimum.

Next (fourth stage), the children's amusement with regard to the adults' mistakes began to decline, and they began to correct the mistakes in a businesslike fashion, without any affectation. The children seemed to be growing used to their new role, seeing nothing unusual in it. But most of them were proud of their equality with the adults and tried to accentuate this both in assignments and outside them. Even the children who were themselves unable to complete an assignment would correctly check the actions of adults and attempt to set them an example. Finally, in the last, fifth stage, the activity of the group evened out rapidly. Whereas earlier a few of the most active children were the principal initiators of corrections, now the situation changed: one by one, the passive children began spontaneously to check their peers and adults and set them an example. The actions of the educator as well as of the assistant became an object of criticism; the models produced by the educator, which earlier had occasioned no comments, were now commented upon by the children ('Is that really a tree? There are a lot of branches on a tree . . .', 'And where is the grass?', 'The sun is red'). In some children, verbal correction was replaced by a tendency to help others: after completing their assignment, they would go to the tables of their slower peers and try to help them.

Another characteristic feature of the experiment was a *dynamic change in children's relation to the assistants*. During the first phase of becoming acquainted, the children's attitude towards the experimenters was restrained; they would answer the experimenter's questions, participate in the fact-finding experiments, but would themselves rarely initiate communication. In addition to curiosity, cautiousness and alienation were sensed in the children's behaviour; some of them refused to participate in the pretests, would not answer questions and cried when an adult began to talk to them.

After the initial lessons, the attitude of most of the children towards the adults became considerably warmer, but it took a month for all the children to become completely used to the new adults. This was reflected most clearly in communication outside the assignments in which initiative shifted completely to the children. Usually, the children would cluster around the assistant before and after the assignments, ask questions, talk about their homework, show new toys and clothes and begin to play.

But the stable, good-natured atmosphere during the experiments, the absence of any manifestations of authority on the part of the experimenters, caused a variety of reactions in the children. Three distinct tendencies were apparent in their attitudes towards the nonauthoritarian adult. The first group chose an outwardly unmotivated, actively negative attitude. The children became aggressive, got along poorly with the adult (they would tug at his or her clothing or hair, crawl on his or her back, hinder him or her from recording the data, etc.), spoke rudely to him or her, threatened to hit, etc. The second group consisted of children who showed a passively positive attitude towards the assistant. They were gentle, smiled, often asked questions and eagerly sought contact. The children in the third group had an actively positive attitude towards the experimenters and showed a strong emotional attachment to some of them: they tried to sit with the assistant during the assignments, and outside the assignments clung to him or her, embraced and kissed him or her, said they loved him or her, etc. Here is an extract from a report in which the behaviour of all three groups is recorded:

> After some mathematics exercises, Renata R. (3 years, 4 months) went up to the experimenter and said, 'And now you know why a cube can't roll?' *Experimenter:* 'Why?' *Renata:* 'Because it is square; it has corners, and they stop it.' Then she said, 'I love you very much' (and embraced him). *Experimenter:* 'Why?' *Renata:* 'Because you help us with our assignments' (embraces him again and says: 'I love you madly'). *Experimenter:* 'Who taught you to say something like that?' *Renata:* 'I thought it up myself, I thought it up myself . . .' Sasha G. (3:3) comes up, with his fists stuck in small wooden barrels. He says sternly to the adult, 'I'm going to kill you with my gloves' (goes away). *Renata:* 'What did he say?' *Experimenter:* 'That he is going to kill me'. Andrei M. (3:6), who had been standing nearby and had heard everything, says with a smile: 'He's just teasing, he's just teasing; you can tease, can't you?' *Renata:* 'I'm going to ask him: I'll go ask him.' She goes up to Sasha G and says: 'You were just teasing that you were going to kill E.V., were you?' *Sasha:* 'Yes.' Renata returns to the adult. 'He was just teasing.'

Usually one of these tendencies predominated in the behaviour of each child, and sometimes they were combined in strange ways. Later, the children's attitudes towards the assistants changed, and by the end of the exercises almost all of the children with 'actively negative' attitudes had shifted to the 'passively positive' group.

Special attention should be paid to *the development of discipline*. During the first days, discipline in the sessions was noticeably reduced. Encountering no stern rebuff from the adults, the children felt free; they stood up in their places, were mischievous, and did not respond to the educator's requests. Classes in physical education were especially difficult. The children reacted to any mistake on the part of an adult with laughter and took it as a signal for merriment: they forgot about order, ran about the room and tumbled about on the floor. It was difficult to get them together and get the class going. Outside the class, the children's play with the adults often had touches of aggression: the children would cling to the adult, pull at his or her clothing, prevent him or her from writing, hang onto his or her shoulders, and would not even respond when the adult asked them to let him or her alone.

By mid-January, the behaviour of the children had changed. Discipline was gradually restored in the classes, and infractions became very rare. This change was especially distinct after a necessary two-week break in the classes because of bad weather. Although they were totally unafraid of the adults, the children began to heed their requests; in physical education, they took the adults' mistakes calmly, and corrected them in turn. Outside the classes, the children did not disturb the adult as he or she wrote in the daybook, and quickly stopped their play with the adult when he or she asked them to; even the aggressive children heeded his or her requests.

One more characteristic worthy of mention is the children's *spontaneous creativity*. Their tendency to modify the models presented to them by the educator and to do something more than was assigned was very distinct from the very first lessons. This tendency was displayed in different ways in different lessons. For example, in lessons in their native language, the children began deliberately to vary the responses: in addition to correct responses, they would give incorrect ones; in guessing games they themselves began to invent riddles. In physical education, after performing the assigned movement, they would begin to vary it.

Spontaneous creativity was especially noticeable in lessons in clay modelling and drawing. After modelling (or drawing) a figure (or a drawing) given to them, the children would frequently add something to it: they would make something out of the remaining pieces of modelling clay, or draw something else on the other side of the sheet of paper. The elements that were not part of the assignment fell clearly into three groups: (1) multiple repetition of the model, (2) introduction of new elements into the assignment and (3) drawing (modelling) new figures not included in the assignment.

As a rule, the children in the experimental groups did not simply do something above and beyond the model but even introduced some new sense into it from their past experience or their fantasy (for instance, if they were asked to draw a schematic model of an automobile, they would draw a driver in the driver's seat, a load in a cart, smoke in chimney, etc.; if they were asked to model a doll, they would put a hat or a crinoline on her, put a basket in her hand, etc.). Other typical innovations were giving a new interpretation to the entire situation, or transforming the assignment from the portrayal of an object to the portrayal of an entire scene; if they were asked to draw a tree, they would also draw other appropriate objects: grass, the sun, flowers, a bird in the tree; if they were asked to model a goat, they would model green grass, trees, flowers, etc. I assume that this enrichment of the situation constitutes the rudiments of the creativity accessible to children of this age. Let me give some examples:

1. The children were asked to model a rabbit. All set about the task assiduously. The assistant was the first to finish the model and said to the educator, 'I am finished.' The educator showed the children the figure made by the adult: 'Children, did E.V. do it right?' Katya T. (4 years 5 months): 'No, he didn't. It doesn't have ears, its paws are short, and it doesn't have a tail.' The assistant attaches pieces of modelling clay to the head of the figure. Igor B. (4.6) looked at the figure and said, 'The ears are too short. That isn't a rabbit; it's a meat pie.' They all laughed. The children examined the objects made by their neighbours, argued and corrected one another. After finishing this job, they began to make other objects. Katya T. made a rabbit, and then a field out of green clay, and flowers; Gelya D. made a rabbit, a flower, and a sun; Igor B. made a rabbit, and then attached second ears to it (a little smaller) and said, 'This is a mother rabbit carrying a baby rabbit . . .'

2. The children are asked to draw a car, and are given a model. They all draw eagerly. The educator shows the children Igor B.'s drawing, which is not too successful, many smile. Gelya D. says, 'That looks like an elephant.' Katya T.: 'Look at that car; it's a house, not a car.' The children discuss the assistant's drawing and make comments. Marina M. (4.3) is the first to add a new element to the drawing: she draws water flowing out of the radiator ('The

water is leaking'), and then adds headlights. Katya T. (4.5) fills the truck with circles and says, 'My car is carrying potatoes.' After this, almost all the children begin to express various ideas: 'I am going to draw a little sun'; 'I'm going to draw the sky and clouds'; 'I'm going to draw the night so that the headlights shine in the dark'; 'My car is a camper; there's a bed and chairs inside it'.

As we see from these examples, the spontaneous creative variations introduced into the assignment flowed organically from the overall emotional atmosphere reigning in the lessons of the experimental group, which in addition to serious activity also contained elements of play and free improvisation. It may be assumed that the originality and potential talent of most children of this age are, in a sense, 'disinhibited' under conditions of a democratic style of social interaction and find broad channels for expression.

As is evident from Figure 2.14 (with numbers of children tested as

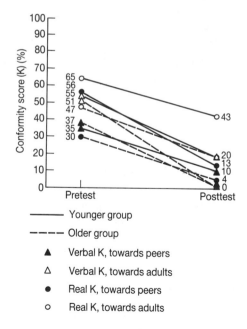

Figure 2.14 Results of pretests and posttests with children in the experimental groups.

follows: younger children tested with a peer partner – 14, and with an adult partner – 17, older children tested with a peer partner – 12, and with an adult partner – 13) and Figure 2.15 (numbers of children as follows: younger children tested with a peer partner – 20, and with an adult partner – 18, older children tested with a peer partner – 17, and with an adult partner – 15), after the formative experiment, in both experimental groups the children's independence had increased considerably in terms of all four parameters. In the control group, independence decreased in terms of all parameters, although the differences were more often not significant.

The coefficient of rank correlation between the children's active engagement in the lessons (correcting the actions of their peers and adults) and changes in the above mentioned four parameters (see Table 2.5) showed that almost all the correlations were either not

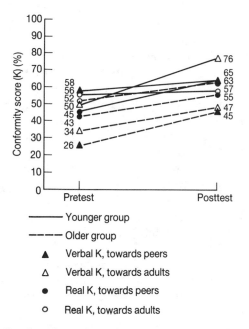

Figure 2.15 Results of pretests and posttests with children in the control groups.

Table 2.5 Correlation of children's active engagement in lessons and changes obtained as a result of a formative experiment

Parameter of change	Younger group			Middle group		
	n	r_s	Level of significance	n	r_s	Level of significance
K_{rp}	14	−0.23	Not significant	12	−0.41	Not significant
K_{vp}	14	0.28	Not significant	12	−0.62	0.05
K_{ra}	17	−0.45	0.5	13	−0.30	Not significant
K_{va}	17	0.01	Not significant	13	−0.58	0.05

Notes: n = number of subjects; r_s = Spearman rank correlation coefficient

significant or negative. This confirms data from observations that children who had demonstrated a high degree of independence in the pretest were the most active in correcting their peers and adults from the first to the last lessons. Conversely, children who had shown high imitation coefficients were passive throughout most of the lessons, and were activated only in the fifth stage of the programme; nevertheless, the most notable changes in the direction of developing independence took place precisely in this group.

We also calculated the coefficients of the spontaneous creativity of children in the experimental and control groups based on parallel test lessons involving clay modelling and drawing (because of their general formlessness, the drawings of the children in the younger groups were not included in the comparison). The dotted line in Figure 2.16 shows the percentage ratio of the average number of elements introduced beyond the assignment to the average number of children present at a lesson (general increment). The unbroken line gives a percentage ratio of the average number of elements not provided in the model to the average number of children present at the lessons (creative extra). The figure indicates that both the general and the creative extras were considerably greater in the experimental groups than in the control groups.

The results reliably confirmed the hypothesis that *the organization of a democratic style of social interaction between adults and children catalyzes in children a tendency towards independent behaviour.* The fact that independent behaviour cultivated in a child using material in classroom lessons was displayed in all 12 test situations indicates that it transfers broadly and warrants our considering it as a quality of the

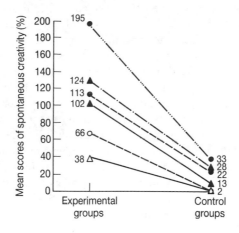

--- Total number of variations in younger groups (○) and older groups (●)
in clay modelling.
——— Number of creative variations in younger groups (△) and older groups (▲)
in clay modelling.
—··— Total number of variations in older groups in drawing.
·—·—· Number of creative variations in older groups in drawing.

Figure 2.16 Mean scores of spontaneous creativity.

child's personality. It was also found that the lessons in the control groups, which were conducted according to an ordinary procedure, produced no increase in children's independent behaviour.

The second important fact was that a democratic style of social interaction heightened children's spontaneous, creative, active involvement in various types of lessons. It may be assumed that such an active involvement is a secondary structure and represents independent actions in different types of activity (drawing, modelling, learning a language, doing physical exercises etc.).

The third fact worthy of attention is the confirmation of a dynamic pattern in the children's attitudes towards the adults who adopted a democratic style of social interaction. Two main stages stand out in this pattern. In the first stage, tolerance towards negative manifestations in the children's behaviour reduced the discipline in the group as a whole, and in some children unleashed negative and aggressive forms of behaviour. Unwavering maintenance of a democratic style of social interaction at this stage required endurance and considerable expenditure of energy on the part of the adult. In the second stage, as if on the rebound, the attitude of the children towards the adults became positive, discipline became normal and aggressive acts disappeared. It should be noted that there was a qualitative difference in the discipline obtained as a result of a democratic style of social interaction from that usually achieved in the authoritarian social interactions: whereas the latter is based mainly on the fear of punishment, the former basically rests on mutual trust and sympathy.

The unique pattern found in the children's attitudes towards democratic adults in certain respects resembled the dynamic pattern described by Lisina (see Lisina, 1986). Their studies showed that the adoption of the friendly communication of a democratic type with children helped to cultivate in them an actively positive attitude towards adults. However, in this study some new features in children's attitudes towards adults were found, in particular a rapid shift from an originally uniformly neutral attitude, through a stage with contrasting poles (fond attachment vs. aggression and negativity), to the transformation of an actively negative attitude into a passively positive attitude. It may be assumed that these characteristics are specific to the democratic style of communication adopted in this study, which, in contrast to a friendly democratic style practised by Lisina, was much more permissive and stressed the equality between children and adults to a greater extent. This style of social interaction was perceived by children as a break in their normal relations with adults, as something 'abnormal', and it produced a variety of reactions, including negative ones that turned into neutral and positive attitudes only later in the study.

It is also interesting that this positive change in children's attitude towards democratic adults was most acutely sensed by the experimenters after the unpredicted two-week break in the lessons in the early January.[5] It may be assumed that the adults, who were unusually patient when the children reacted negatively towards them, became necessary to them, and that the 'loss' of such adults, even a temporary one, was sorely felt by the children, arousing in them a sympathetic feeling and creating a positive attitude towards the adults.

One problem with this study, however, is that attaining this alteration of the status differential between adults and children requires constant (weekly) changes in the traditional roles. The attendant demands placed on teachers, including a restructuring of their typical attitudes and habitual styles of interaction with children is both difficult and emotionally draining. Clearly, it is easier for teachers to work in the traditional authoritarian style.

Thus, the main goals of Experiment 2 were to determine first whether a 'mixed' style, in which the teacher retained her traditional role while the experimenter's assistant took on the pupil role, would lead to an increase in the independence displayed to the assistant similar to that attained in the previous experiment, and second, whether the independence attained would transfer to the more traditional teacher (Subbotsky, in print).[6]

Two regular preschool classes were used as the experimental group (30 4-year-olds) and the control group (34 same-age children). Both groups consisted of ethnically and socioeconomically mixed populations. The teachers were middle-aged females, professional preschool teachers, and the assistants were two female university students.

The procedure in this study was basically the same as before. The major difference between this study and the previous one, in which the teacher and the assistant changed roles each week so that both functioned in turn as the 'ideal model for emulation' and the 'children's partner', was that in this study the teacher retained her traditional role and practised authoritarian control (punishments, reprimands, rewards, direct encouragement, and so on). The role of 'children's partner' was taken only by the assistant.

Lessons were conducted in this fashion three times a week for four months. The types and number of lessons were as follows: drawing (11 times), modelling (10), Russian language (10), mathematics (5), physical education (6), design (4), appliqué work (6), for a total of 52 lessons. In the control group the same lessons were carried out, with slight variations, using the traditional teaching style. The assistant was present at the lessons but did not take part in them.

The pre- and posttests were administered to each child in the experimental and control groups before and after the four-month treatment. For the experimental group these tests were identical to those described in the 'screening experiment', including both verbal and actual behaviour, and the screening–nonscreening conditions. For the control group only one of the experimental conditions (no screening) was used in the pre- and posttests.

In the course of this educationally oriented study we found results very similar to those described earlier. However, as opposed to what was found in the previous experiment, there was no initial reduction and later gradual restoration of discipline; the children remained equally disciplined for the entire experimental procedure, the discipline, however, being of rather an authoritarian type. The children's spontaneous activity (their tendency to modify the models presented to them by the teacher and do more than was assigned) was displayed very clearly in the experimental group, although in this study it was not formally measured.

Comparison of pretests and posttests revealed that a significant increase in independent behaviour was found in the experimental group only (see Figure 2.17), although the initial level of independence in the control group was slightly lower than in the experimental group. The comparison of Ks under the various experimental conditions (only relevant for the experimental group) revealed neither 'screening effect' nor 'partner effect'.

These data indicate that employing this 'mixed' style of interaction led to a considerable increase in the children's independence, comparable to that achieved in the previous experiment. In addition, the independence that emerged in interactions with the assistant who reduced her status level to that of the children was transferred towards the teacher who continued to behave in traditional fashion.

As was also found in earlier research, there was a steady transition from surprise and perplexity in the adult's responses to correction in a businesslike fashion. The dynamics of the children's attitude towards

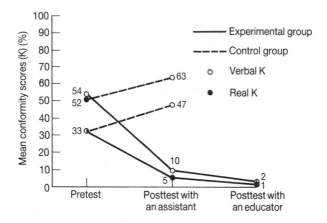

Figure 2.17 Results of pretests and posttests under 'no screening' conditions.

the assistant was similar too – from alienation at the beginning to a positive emotional attitude at the end. However, unlike the previous study's findings, there were no displays of the exaggerated (sometimes aggressive, sometimes over-friendly) behaviours towards the adults. Whereas in the previous study discipline declined at times, in this study there was no such decline, no doubt due to the presence and influence of the teacher, who retained her traditional teaching style. Nevertheless, despite all the changes in the behaviour of the teacher, we found that the independence shown by the children to the assistant was transferred to the teacher as well. Perhaps the mere presence of the teacher during the course of the assistant–child interactions was enough to achieve a linking of the two people – the children had clear indications that the teacher was willing to go along with this a-typical behaviour.

Finally, we should note that there was no screening effect during either the pre- or posttests. This signifies that those children who were independent in the pretest (as well as those who became independent or retained their independence in the posttest) were independent not because of fear of the experimenter's disapproval but because of some inner need 'to fulfil the correct programme'.

A sketch of the development of independent behaviour in preschoolers

As was mentioned earlier, the emergence of the elements of independent behaviour in preschool children's behaviour is an important landmark in their psychological development. The major significance of this newly formed capacity is in that it crucially changes the way the children assimilate social experience: from global imitation of social models they progress to the selective assimilation of those types of behaviour that correspond with the programmes they had assimilated earlier and the refusal of those that do not.

Indeed, as both observations and experiments show, any programme (norm) assimilated by a young child can easily be substituted by another (and even a contrasting) programme (norm) as soon as the child has an opportunity to observe the different programmes (norms): the diffuse and global character of the assimilation is, therefore, a 'negative side' of its high sensitivity. In contrast, a preschool child absorbs the contradictive social influences to a lesser extent than does the young child; and at the same time his or her resistance to the influence of the incorrect actions or opinions of other people increases.

The facts that testify in favour of the presence of initial forms of independent behaviour in young preschoolers were observed in diary studies (Mukhina, 1969), and in some other studies this type of behaviour was made a subject of psychological enquiry (see, for instance, Hamm and Hoving, 1969, 1970). However, in these studies the structure of conformative and independent behaviour in children was analyzed insufficiently. Besides, according to the broadly accepted view independence (interpreted as nonconformity) first emerges at a relatively advanced age (in schoolchildren and in adolescents). In contrast, the most valuable quality of the young preschooler's personality is sometimes viewed in its general imitativeness, in the preschool child's belief in adult's infallibility. Consequently, education in nurseries and in primary schools is often arranged in the form of an authoritarian social contact in which the educator shows only one side of him/herself to the child: that of an ideal bearer of social experience, a model for global imitation. His/her other side, which is part of any person – vacillations, doubts and mistakes – is carefully concealed from the child.

However, our experimental studies have shown that elements of independence in behaviour take shape even in young preschoolers. They first appear in the sphere of verbal behaviour and verbal assessment of the actions of others, and then, somewhat later, in the domain of actual deeds. The child first displays independence relative to his or her peers, and then relative to adults. His or her transition from global imitative to independent behaviour presumes not only (and not so much as) the development of his or her intelligence but the development of his or her personality, which is gradually being released from a GIA to people. This liberation sets in when the child is periodically switched from the position of pupil and imitator to that of teacher and controller of the actions of adults.

Experimental analysis of the conforming behaviour under the 'partner screening' condition allowed us to reject the hypothesis that this behaviour was due to a fear of the partner's disapproval (Experiment 1). Our findings suggest, instead, that in the standard experimental situation preschoolers imitated the partner's incorrect actions because they considered him or her to be an infallible person (a motive for global imitation).

Hiding all but the experimenter's hands (the screening condition) suggested that independent behaviour in the standard experimental situation cannot be explained by the experimenter's indirect influence (Experiment 2). The absence of any screening effect makes the hypothesis of independence based on self-esteem appear more likely. These data do not support the view that independent behaviour is merely the reversed imitation of the experimenter's actions by the child, as under the screening condition imitation of this kind should disappear.

All the data brought me to the conclusion that it is not the development (or lack) of certain intellectual skills that plays a crucial role in the children's ability to reveal independent (nonconforming) behaviour, but rather the change in the emotional attitude towards people rooted in the child's social position in a society.

It was assumed that psychological mechanisms through which this social position can influence the children's consciousness is the 'style of social interaction'; namely, the authoritarian style fosters the GIA in children, whereas a democratic style prompts the development of independent behaviour.

A special series of experiments in which children were subjected to the influence of both of the above mentioned styles of social interaction strongly confirmed the hypothesis. The experiments clearly showed that in order to facilitate independence in children the traditional authoritarian style of social interaction that prevails in a classroom should be modified and, where possible, replaced by the democratic style of interaction.

Consequently, research was conducted that suggested that the development of independence in a preschool group could indeed be fostered in a classroom in which traditional patterns of authority were altered by adults (an assistant and a teacher) in turn occupying the roles of 'teacher' and 'child'.

The second important fact yielded in this study was that a democratic style of social interaction heightened children's spontaneous, creative, active involvement. It may be assumed that this spontaneous, active involvement is a secondary structure and represents the concrete 'shell' that surrounds independent actions in different types of activity (drawing, modelling, learning a language, doing physical exercises, etc.)

Yet the research showed that the application of DSI in its 'pure' form, along with positive effect, also produces certain negative results, such as a liberation of aggressive tendencies in children and the relaxation of discipline. Unwavering maintenance of DSI is fairly time consuming and requires endurance and a considerable expenditure of energy on the part of the adult. These disadvantages may be avoided if a 'mixed' style of social interaction is applied. The data of the last experiment indicated that similar results but without their negative accompanying effects could be achieved through a 'mixed' pattern of interaction, in which the role change was made only by the assistant, while the teacher continued to behave in traditional fashion. The independence that was displayed by the children to the assistant was transferred to the traditional teacher.

In general, the research reviewed in this chapter prompts one to create a certain hypothesis of how independent behaviour might develop in preschool-age children in real life.

Since the necessary prerequisite for the independent action is a certain degree of intellectual maturity (the knowledge of certain programmes, the ability to compare these programmes with other people's actions, a certain degree of voluntary behaviour) the development of these abilities may be viewed as *the first stage* of the arising of independence in children. There are certain grounds to update this period to early childhood (from 0 to 3 years approximately).

Indeed, the numerous studies show that it is just at this period that children's increased intellectual abilities allow them to acquire a number of complex programmes: language, actions with human artifacts, certain social norms (e.g. toilet training), etc. (see El'konin, 1960; Garrison, 1968; Mussen, Conger and Kagan, 1979; Cole and Cole, 1989). It is in this period that the first form of voluntary behaviour emerges and children acquire the capacity to create plans and programmes of their future behaviours (Bruner, 1973; Luria, 1971; Luria and Subbotsky, 1978). The acquisition of these cognitive and voluntary capacities, together with the growth of children's experience, creates a basis that makes independent behaviour possible and gives the children a measure against which they can compare people's performance.

However, the acquisition of these capacities, being a necessary premise for the development of independence, is in no way sufficient. Both observations and experiments (see the previous paragraph) show that at this age independent (nonconformative) actions can be observed but very rarely. The children's behaviour becomes more autonomous (they gradually acquire such abilities as crawling and walking, eating without help, dressing themselves, etc.) but they still tend to imitate adult and peer's actions globally as far as it concerns the programmed behaviour (and not just caprices or whims).

The cause for that, in my view, is the social position that the child of this age occupies in his or her relations with adults. On the one hand, the gap between the child's and the adult's intellectual and physical capacities is yet so big that the child inevitably has to give a leading role to an adult and to leave the role of an imitator for him or herself. On the other hand, due to the adult's intellectual superiority he or she is necessarily put in the position of 'norm-giving subject', a leader and a controller. The relationships between a child and the adult are inevitably unilateral, the adult being 'a teacher' and the child 'a pupil'. Besides, because the child of this age is taught basically by certain close and 'significant' persons (parents, older siblings), the programmes he or she learns have a 'personalized' character, i.e. they are 'merged' in the child's consciousness with the personal image of their 'owner'. This makes the comparison between the programmes and the close adults' actions particularly difficult, even if possible, for the child.

It may be assumed that it is just these factors that create in the child's mind the GIA towards adults. This, mainly unconscious, attitude accounts for the fact that the child conforms to erroneous actions of adults (and sometimes of peers as well) even if he or she under different conditions can do the programme well. This attitude is a sort of 'affective' emotional disposition, since many children persist in their global imitative behaviour even if they are completely aware of the adults' mistakes and can correct them verbally.

One may conclude, therefore, that the next stage in the development of independence is the overcoming of the GIA by the child. Since the GIA is supposed to be a consequence of the child's submissive position in his or her unilateral social interactions with adults, the dissipation of this attitude should be expected to occur when the child is gradually involved in those types of activities in which he or she can feel his or her equality with adults. Cooperative activities (role play, verbal discussion, all sorts of shared activities) exercise exactly those functions.

Indeed, it is in a cooperative activity that a child and an adult interact as equal partners: they must both subordinate their actions to the same rule and must exercise control over each other's actions. Within the bilateral interaction the adult is no longer a norm-giving subject, his or her actions are no longer identified with the rules and norms in their own right. It is in this type of activities that the adult is perceived by the child for the first time as an individual who can make errors and, what is even more psychologically important, whose errors the child is supposed (and obliged) not to follow. No wonder, therefore, that the involvement in cooperative activities may gradually weaken and discount the adult's 'infallibility' in the child's mind and destroy the GIA.

As is well known, the role of cooperative activities in children's intellectual development was stressed by many scholars, in particular by Piaget and Vygotsky. Piaget viewed cooperation between children as an essential factor in the development of logical operations, on the one hand, and autonomous moral reasoning, on the other hand, that first take shape at the stage of concrete operations (from 7 to 11–12 years old) (Piaget, 1954); Vygotsky made emphasis on cooperation between children and adults in which a zone of proximal development is created (Vygotsky, 1987). However, both theories concentrated on the role cooperative activities have for children's cognitive development, whereas in this study emphasis is made on their role in the development of children's emotional attitude towards adults. The results of the study allow us to assume that cooperative activities began to play this important role long before children reach the age of 7 and, in fact, within the Piagetian preoperational period. It seems plausible to assume that a few years before cooperative activities start to produce an effect upon children's intellectual development they have already begun to undermine and weaken the children's original GIA towards adults.

This weakening eliminates the final obstacle for emergence of independent behaviour; however, it does not automatically create a positive motivation for independence. In other words, even if the child now does not feel obliged to follow models' erroneous actions, what makes the child opt for the right way of doing the programmes and waive the wrong ones is still an open question. As was assumed earlier, there may be two major forms of independent behaviour motivation. First, the child can decide on the earlier assimilated programmes merely because of a fear of punishment by the authoritative persons who imposed these programmes on him or her. This type of behaviour can be called 'independent' only with a certain degree of approximation since independence from the deviative models turns out here to be a dependence on the initial authorities (parents, relatives, etc.). This type of independence (earlier I called it 'pragmatic independence') is initiated by the external control and it is of little interest for psychological analysis.

However, the child may opt for the earlier assimilated programmes, not just because of fear of punishment but because he/she is aware of the 'rightness' of the programme that he/she assimilated earlier. This feeling of 'rightness', being incorporated into the child's self-esteem (i.e. in the positive image of him/herself as of a person doing right things), may create an intrinsic motivation for independent behaviour. It was assumed that such an intrinsic motivation for independence can arise as a result of the democratic style of social interaction that is also a crucial factor in creating the child's positive self-image. As a consequence, the child may become independent not only in his or her verbal judgements, but in his or her practical actions as well.

It was also assumed that a psychological basis for the transition from predominantly authoritarian to a democratic style of social interaction in the relationships between children and adults is the fundamental shift that these relationships undergo in this period, i.e. the shift from mainly unilateral activities to cooperative activities in interactions between children and adults. Since this transition covers mainly the preschool and primary school ages (from 3 to 7 or 8) in which cooperative types of activities first appear and occupy a legitimate position in the relationships between children and adults (see El'konin, 1978; Cole and Cole, 1989), this age may be viewed as *a second stage in the development of independent behaviour.*

This stage presumably has its peak at the end of the fourth year of life. It is at this age that children's imitative behaviour with respect to their peer partners' mistakes almost disappears and there is a maximal increase of children displaying independent behaviour with respect to an adult partner's actions. The fact that the independence first emerges in children with respect to their peers and only later is it followed by independence with respect to adults can be explained by the different proportion of cooperative-type activities in these two domains of relationships. Indeed, in the children's relationships with their peers cooperative activities play a greater role than in their relationships with adults, therefore the GIA fades faster and earlier towards peers than it fades towards adults.

Lastly, an important characteristic of the second stage of independence development is that it first appears in the sphere of verbal judgements and only later is followed by independence in actual behaviour. Although this phenomenon can be caused by a number of factors, two of them (one general and the other specific to preschool-age children) seem to play a major role here. First, as was stressed earlier, verbal behaviour basically possesses a much greater degree of reversibility, requires a lesser degree of commitment from an acting person and is, therefore, less risky than actual behaviour; it is, therefore, easier for a person to act independently in his/her words that in his/her deeds. Second, the cooperative-type activities in preschoolers' communications with their peers and adults normally appear first in their verbal communications (verbal arguing, verbal corrections) and only after this, somewhat later, in their actual behaviourial interactions (role play, cooperative labour activities, etc.). As a consequence, the GIA fades and disappears first from the sphere of children's verbal interactions with their peers and adults and only after this from the sphere of real behaviour.

Of course, this picture of the development of independence is nothing but a rough approximation of what really occurs. First, the transition from globally imitative to independent behaviour is basically incomplete: it covers only a certain group of programmes that children of this age can do well. Second, independent behaviour in a preschool child is not yet a stable psychological quality: it may well be replaced by global imitation if the child is subjected to a strong authoritarian influence. Despite all this, the early stages of the development of independent behaviour have a fundamental importance, since they constitute the first step the child makes towards becoming a matured personality.

The other side of this process is the development of moral behaviour in the child. It is assumed in this book that moral development occurs at one time with the development of independence and creates a potential 'counterweight' to independence. Although these two personality qualities play different (perhaps, opposite) roles in the adjustment of an individual to his or her society, it may well happen that they share certain social determinants for getting their development off the ground. This assumption gains support in the study in which a relationship between 4–6-year-old children's independence to an adult and the intentionality of their moral judgements was found (Helkama, 1987). To consider this possibility is the purpose of the next chapter.

Notes

1. Comparable data were yielded in a study made with Finnish children of 4 to 6 years old in which the experimental paradigm described (children's behaviour in a joint action with an adult partner) was employed (Helkama, 1987).

2. From now on the terms 'independence' or 'independent behaviour' will mean intrinsically motivated 'unpragmatic' independence, unless mentioned specifically.

3. Since voluntary capacity (that is capacity to overcome an original tendency to imitate any stimuli available in the perceptual field) is mainly rooted in physiology and neurodynamics (see Luria and Subbotsky, 1978), it is not susceptible to external intervention. Consequently, in this study only the children who had manifested a necessary level of 'voluntary maturity' participated, the sufficient criteria for this being their ability to perform conflict programmes together with a peer partner.

4. In some of my articles I refer to this style as to the 'altruistic style' in order to stress that an adult voluntarily refuses here from his or her legitimate right to exercise control over children's actions.

5. Because of the severe cold, the heating system in the kintergarten stopped functioning and the kintergarten was closed.

6. The study was conducted by the author in cooperation with his students, T. A. Semenova and T. I. Lucashevitch.

Chapter 3

The Moral Development of the Preschool Child

Moral judgement and moral conduct

Since the phenomenon of moral behaviour, as well as that of independent behaviour, is complex, the first task in studying moral development is to distinguish between the main structural components of moral behaviour. My first distinction is between the form and content of a moral act. With regard to *form*, a moral act may take place either as verbal or as actual (real) behaviour. The term *verbal behaviour*, as it was defined in Chapter 1, will be used to mean subjects' abstract, theoretical judgement about how they would or should behave in imaginary situations involving a moral conflict. Within this formulation, moral conflicts require a choice between an egoistic act and a prosocial act (or an act for the good of others). In contrast to the term *verbal behaviour* I use the term *actual behaviour* to refer to acts that take place in situations containing an actual moral conflict in which subjects are personally involved.

The *content* of moral acts also can be distinguished. I distinguish between pragmatic and nonpragmatic moral acts. A *pragmatic moral act* is a behaviour that is carried out in accordance with a moral norm and is guided by a social incentive or by the fear of punishment for diverging from moral norms. In contrast, *nonpragmatic moral acts* are not motivated by external controls exerted by other people. Rather, nonpragmatic acts are those that reflect subjects' preservation of their moral self-esteem or principles.

Investigation of moral behaviour in psychology includes a vast range of studies. The majority of these studies are concentrated on the development of moral judgements (the cognitive approach of Piagetian–Kohlbergian perspective). A theoretical basis for this approach was laid by Piaget's study of the development of children's moral judgements (Piaget, 1957). According to Piaget, moral development is one part of the more general process of the child's *adaptation* to his or her social milieu. A characteristic feature of Piaget's theory is the assumption that there is a certain correspondence between children's intellectual development and the development of their 'moral feelings' (Piaget, 1954). This assumption is based upon the premise that the development of both cognitive and 'affectivity' domains is determined by changes in children's 'behaviourial schemes': the stable predispositions to respond to certain situations in a similar way. The schemes can be generalized to cover and organize the child's actions with the external objects, on the one hand, and his or her relationships with people, on the other.

Moral feelings first appear in children in a preoperational stage of intellectual development (from 2 to 7 years of age). Due to the absence of 'operations' (the reversible interiorized systems of intellectual actions) in this stage children's thinking is captured by the perceptual field and is unable to grasp the intrinsic properties of things. The well-known manifestation of this characteristic is the inability of a preoperational child to solve problems on conservation of various properties (quantity, matter, volume, number, etc.) of things as the things change their forms. The other characteristic of preoperational thinking is its 'fracturedness' – the absence of a unified and universal approach to various domains of reality.

Similar characteristics exist in the domain of moral judgements (Piaget, 1957). In this stage (the stage of 'moral realism' in Piaget's terms) children's moral judgements are not yet generalized. Thus, the children know that to lie is a bad thing to do, however they believe that lying to peers is 'less bad' than lying to adults. The other feature of the 'moral realism' judgements is that they are determined by the 'apparent' rather than the 'essential' properties in human relations. For instance, trying to decide which of two boys should be given a worse punishment – the boy who broke 10 cups inadvertently or the boy who committed an offence and broke a cup while doing this – preoperational children are inclined to prescribe a stronger punishment for the first boy; thus, in their 'punishment distribution' they rely on the magnitude of the material damage caused by the boys and not on their intrinsic motivation. In this stage children are likely to interpret all the adults' requirements as moral laws; the latter are not yet distinguished from the former as something universal and independent of human intentions. At the same time, the children are prone to believe in 'immanent justice': they would think, for instance, that a story character who committed an offence and later fell down into the brook suffered the misfortune because he was guilty and not for natural reasons. Piaget describes this level of morality as 'morality of authoritarianism and submission' that is based on the unilateral respect children of this age feel towards adults.

In the next stage (the stage of 'concrete operations') that lasts from approximately 7 to 12 years of age, children's intelligence acquires reversibility; now they are able to go beyond the external properties of things towards their essential characteristics. Thus, they can easily manage conservation problems and take into account the fact that certain parameters of things remain unchanged while their shapes change. These improved intellectual capacities are reflected in children's moral judgements, which are described by Piaget as 'the morality of equality and mutual respect'. On the one hand, the children no longer consider moral laws as something 'divine', and their belief in 'immanent justice' fades; on the other, moral laws become generalized and independent of varying circumstances. Thus, in their 'punishment distribution judgements' the children no longer rely on the magnitude of the material damage but give priority to the story characters' intentions.

At last, in the formal operational stage (from 12 to 14–15 years of age) children's thinking is able to leave the concrete ground behind; it does not need the support of physical objects' and relies entirely upon symbols. Similar transformations occur in children's moral feelings, which, Piaget believes, are reflected in their moral judgements: they lose their inter-individual character and turn into the feelings to 'society as a whole'. Teenagers are able to distinguish 'moral reality' as a set of universal laws and to meditate on this reality theoretically.

Piaget's book generated several groups of studies. The first group scrutinized Piaget's claim that there was a positive relationship between cognitive development and the development of moral judgements. Thus, Lerner (1938) traced the dynamics of the egocentricity of children's moral judgements and found that these judgements become less egocentric with age. In other studies the maturity of children's moral judgements was compared with the levels of their intellectual development; in some of them (Durkin, 1959; Loughran, 1966) the relationship was not observed, whereas in others (Ambron and Irvine, 1975; Barkley, 1942; Damon, 1975) it was. Hardeman (1972) found a significant relationship between the maturity of children's operational structures and their moral judgements.

In the second group of studies Piaget's moral dilemmas were modified and applied to children of more advanced ages than those Piaget referred to. In some of these studies the relativity of the age borderlines between the stages of moral reasoning was demonstrated (Kay, 1969; Loughran, 1957). It was found that many teenagers, along with judgements of higher levels, reveal judgements pertained to the 'moral realism' level. The most well-known and elaborate set of studies within this group is that by Kohlberg, who developed his own variation of moral dilemmas and gave a different (from that of Piaget) description of the stages of moral reasoning (Kohlberg, 1976). Kohlberg distinguished six stages in the development of moral judgements, which are based on three levels of moral orientation: the premoral level (stages 1 and 2), in which one's notions of good and bad are purely pragmatic and derive from the desire to obtain reward and to avoid punishment, the conventional level (stages 3 and 4), where moral virtues are judged as based on the 'sense of duty' and loyalty to authority, and morality is viewed as a kind of convention between the person and the authority; and the postconventional level (stages 5 and 6), in which moral standards gradually become internally controlled, individual principles related to universal moral laws (such as the Golden Rule, for instance, which prescribes that a person should treat others in the same way as he or she would like to be treated by them). The studies by Kohlberg and those who used his Moral Judgement Scale revealed certain similarities, as well as differences, in the development of moral judgements among teenagers and adults in various social and cultural settings (Berkowitz and Gibbs, 1985; Boyes and Walker, 1988; Glover and Steele, 1990; Helkama and Ikonen, 1986; Kohlberg and Kramer, 1969; Maqsud and Rouhani, 1990).

The cognitive approach has been a major trend in studies of moral development during recent decades (for more extensive reviews, see DePalma and Foley, 1975; Likona, 1976; Rushton, 1980; Staub, 1984). In many of the studies Piaget's and Kohlberg's findings were developed and scrutinized. Thus, in the studies of retributive justice dealing with the question of moral responsibility and the blame-worthiness of an agent for the harm he or she caused to someone else it was shown that 6- and 7-year-old children are already able to view intentional harm as more blameworthy than accidental harm (Karniol, 1978; Ferguson and Rule, 1983). In another group of studies, children's judgements about distributive justice were further analyzed (see Damon, 1981, for the review). Thus, Lerner (1974) showed that kindergarten-age children mainly followed the rule of equal distribution of the reward between themselves and their partners, independently of the 'personal contribution' they had made to the work done together. Children of the 5th grade also distributed the reward according to the 'parity' principle, although their tendency to distribute prize stickers according to personal contribution was more salient – perhaps because of the lack of emphasis on the fact that the children worked in a 'team' rather than as 'co-workers' that was made in the first experiment. In some of the studies, children of 5 and even younger were found to be able to use the equality rule in reward distribution (Hook and Cook, 1979). However, distributive judgements depended on the children's socioeconomic status with the children from lower socioeconomic status families being less likely to give 'equality judgements' than their peers from middle SES families (Enright *et al.*, 1980).

Some of the studies of moral judgements focused on the roles of social and cultural contexts in children's learning of moral rules. It was found in a series of observational studies that children learn moral rules from their caregivers (adults) and older siblings in a nondirectional way, so that the caregivers only occasionally give the children direct moral teaching (Dunne and Munn, 1987; Edwards, 1980, 1987). The other characteristic of this learning is that moral rules are most often mixed with all sorts of other constraints and prohibitions so that children may easily confuse them. In his extensive comparative study of moral judgments in the US and in the USSR Bronfenbrenner (1970) revealed the relationships of schoolchildren's moral judgements with the broad social context of children's life, in particular with the individualistic orientation of the US cultural tradition and the more collectivistically oriented education in Russia. The question was left open, however, as to whether the differences in children's moral judgements could be taken as reliable indicators of the corresponding differences in their real behaviour: collectivistic statements may well not go beyond mere declarations. Other studies employed Kohlberg's scale in order to examine the.role of cultural context in the development of children's moral judgements (see Shweder *et al.*, 1987). Most studies showed that in certain groups of people who continue to live a traditional life in isolated villages moral judgements are mostly limited by stage 3 (Edwards, 1982; Kohlberg, 1969; Tietjen and Walker, 1985) – a finding that Kohlberg linked to the insufficient development of formal logical reasoning in these groups of people (Kohlberg, 1984).

In the studies described above the limits of the cognitive approach to studies of moral development became more and more obvious. On the one hand, Piaget's results were assumed to be, in part, biased by specific characteristics of his moral dilemmas (Gabennesch, 1990; Jose, 1990). On the other hand, it was pointed out that the development of moral judgements is not necessarily accompanied by the appropriate moral behaviour (Kay, 1969; Darley and Shultz, 1990): thus, Rushton's (1976) review of studies on altruism showed a rather low correlation of children's altruistic behaviour across situations and did not provide the reader with unequivocal evidence of positive relationships between moral judgements and altruistic behaviour. Some investigators point out that whereas real behaviour has more solid roots in children's motivations and dispositions, moral judgements are rather fragile and can be changed by the mere exposure to models (Bandura and MacDonald, 1963; Sternlieb and Youniss, 1975).

The last claim receives major support from the 'social learning' approach to morality that was developed within social learning theory as an alternative to the cognitive developmental approach. According to social learning theorists, moral behaviour cannot be satisfactorily explained by postulating various hypothetical agents in the human mind, such as 'consciousness', 'superego', or 'cognitive schemes'. The mere fact that a person can uphold moral rules even if he or she cannot make mature moral judgements testifies against the cognitive developmental view. Rather, moral consciousness is an anxiety response to certain specific types of situations and actions (Eysenk, 1960; Skinner, 1971). If a child breaks a certain moral norm, he or she is likely to be punished; the anxiety evoked by the repeated punishments gradually 'sticks' to the behaviours and prevents their reappearance in the child's behaviourial repertoire, whereas following the moral rule becomes the norm since it is positively reinforced.

In contrast to the ideologists of the classical conditioning scheme in moral development, other social learning theorists proposed a refined interpretation of the behaviourial conditioning methodology (Bandura and Walters, 1964; Mowrer, 1950). They point out that the punishment of children for violation of a certain norm alone cannot explain why the children start to behave *in accordance* with the norm and do not simply shift to other (as yet unpunished) forms of violations. Where do new forms of behaviour in the child's behaviourial repertoire come from? The answer is: from 'observational learning', i.e. from children's imitation of adults' words and deeds. In a series of studies Bandura and Walters (1964) showed that the observation of models (in particular, models demonstrating aggressive behaviour) does elicit imitation in children. Later studies in which children observed models demonstrating moral reasoning yielded contradictive results: in some it was found that the observation of moral behaviour facilitates similar behaviour in subjects (Wagner and Wheeler, 1969), in others no increase in subjects' 'prosocial behaviour' was observed (Harris *et al.*, 1973; Harris and Samerott, 1975).

The third influential perspective in the studies of moral development has its roots in psychoanalysis. Freud himself viewed moral development as a part of the gradual replacement of the 'pleasure principle' by the 'reality principle' (Freud, 1966). In this development three main phases were distinguished. In the first (oral) phase an infant finds satisfaction of its sexual drives through sucking and possessing its mother's breast. After the child is deprived of breast feeding the second (anal) phase begins, during which the child's erotic drive is satisfied through excretion processes. At the age of 4 or 5 years the child enters the third major phase. At this (genital) phase the child's sexual drive is already fixed on a parent of the opposite sex.

Children come across the first requirements of reality in their second phase: here the requirements are mild and basically concentrated around toilet training. In the third phase the demands and prohibitions of reality, including moral prohibitions, come through all the domains of the child's life. At the beginning, a major determinant of the child's adaptation to reality is his or her helplessness and dependence on adults. Being unable to gratify his or her needs independently the child has to accept all the adult's requirements. This process is described in terms of 'imitation' and 'identification' (S. Freud, 1966; A. Freud, 1965). The child identifies him/herself with the adult's requirements and a series of changes occurs in his or her personality: the development of voluntary and mediated perception and memory, the development of speech and logical thinking, the development of self-regulation and self-control. A set of these changes is viewed as the first step in a socialization process that finds its climax in the emergence of the 'Ego' – a summary result of the mediation and integration of psychological functions.

The development of the Ego allows a subject to delay and postpone the development of his of her personal needs, but it cannot explain moral behaviour. Indeed, criminal and immoral personalities sometimes are able to reveal sophisticated voluntary behaviour and self-control that are applied, however, to reach antisocial and immoral goals. That is why, in Freud's view, the true moral development only starts at the point where the Ego development is completed. Moral development is a special process of 'introjection' of parents' moral norms by a child. As a result, a system of intrinsic moral criteria (a censorship) develops and solidifies in a special unity called 'superego'. The force behind the introjection is the 'Oedipus complex' – the erotic drive a child has to his or her parent of the opposite sex. Since the child is unable to eliminate his or her 'rival' (a parent of the same sex) physically, he or she solves the problem by identifying him/herself with the 'rival' and through this, with the moral standards the parent represents. Superego is, therefore, described as an intrinsic controller that guarantees moral behaviour's autonomy and independence from external control.

Of course, there is a variety of views on the process of moral development among the representatives of the psychoanalytical approach (see, for instance, Horney, 1950; Sullivan, 1953). Sometimes moral development is viewed in a simplistic way as the development of the Ego only (see, for example, Alexander and Staub, 1931). However, it is just this simplistic interpretation that seems to inspire a vast range of studies that emerge 'on the borderline' between the social learning and psychoanalytical approaches. Thus, Mowrer distinguished two types of identification in the works of Sigmund and Anna Freud: the 'primary identification' (the first 3–4 years of life) and 'defensive identification'. In his studies Mowrer used a social learning perspective to explain the development of primary identification (Mowrer, 1950).

Although the mechanisms of the defensive identification cannot be examined as easily as those of the primary one, some scholars tried to check up certain consequences to which the existence of the defensive identification could lead. In Sears *et al.*'s studies (1965), most of such consequences were not confirmed. The difficulties with the confirmation of the role of defensive identification reflect the general flaw of the psychoanalytical approach to moral development – its basically hypothetical, nonempirical orientation which is very difficult to verify in experimental research.

From relatively recently developed perspectives one of the most known is that which links the development of moral and prosocial behaviour with the development of empathy. Thus, Hoffman (1975, 1988) in his 'empathy scheme' views motivation of moral behaviour as a result of empathic distress and other empathy-based affects. According to this author, children in their first year of life are able to feel only a global empathic distress if they witness another person's suffering (the first level of empathy development). In so far as children's cognitive abilities grow (a second year of life) they become able to differentiate between their own 'self' and that of another person. Consequently, their empathy becomes more differentiated and directed toward another person, however, it is still 'egocentric', since children do not yet understand that the other person in distress may have different feelings from their own (the second level). With a further development of cognitive abilities (in particular, a role-taking ability) children's empathy loses its egocentric character: they can now understand that another person's feelings may be different from their own and react in a way more appropriate to the other person's feelings (the third level). At last, on the fourth level (which children do not normally reach until late childhood), they are able to make a rather sophisticated 'emotional analysis' of another person's feelings in a distress situation; in their empathic responses they can now take into consideration not only the immediate position of a suffering person, but also his or her social position, whether the distress is transitional or chronic, etc. Thus, in Hoffman's scheme, as in Piaget's, cognitive and emotional components in moral behaviour are tied together, but this time they are viewed more like two sides of a single whole rather than as two separate processes.

The empathic approach touches upon a sensitive point in an old theoretical discussion on the nature of moral motivation, in which two major positions may be outlined. One is that of Adam Smith (1966), who considered empathy to be the only motive for true morality. In his view, empathy forces a person to uphold moral laws even in the absence of external control or the pressure of social environment (see

Batson, 1990, for the modern interpretation and the empirical confirmation). The second position is represented by Kant (1965b), who stressed the egoistic nature of empathy. According to Kant, true (i.e. autonomous) morality can be based solely on intellectual understanding (awareness) of one's moral duty and not on feeling of any kind, including empathic feeling.

In a number of empirical studies it was found that empathic feelings facilitated moral and altruistic behaviours (Aronfreed, 1968; Bryan, 1971; Staub, 1971; Roe, 1980; Yarrow *et al.*, 1973). Others argue that empathy improves only verbal altruism (Eisenberg-Berg and Lennon, 1980; Knudson and Kagan, 1982). The question on the role of empathy is complicated by the complexity of the concept itself: as well as moral behaviour, empathy has cognitive and emotional components, and there are various kinds of empathy and sympathy (Hoffman, 1983). Recent studies showed that only affective (emotional) components of empathy were significantly related to children's prosocial behaviour (Lennon *et al.*, 1986; Eisenberg *et al.*, 1987). As was found in Eisenberg and Miller's review (1987), questionnaire measures of empathy were positively related to the prosocial behaviour of children and adults, as well as self-reports of empathy in simulated experiments, whereas picture/story indices of empathy were not. One possible explanation for the discrepancy between the results of experiments with picture/story indices and those involving experimental simulations or experimental inductions was that in the former the objects of the subject's empathy and of their prosocial actions were different, whereas in the latter they were usually the same. This explanation may be viewed as evidence in favour of the claim that empathy-evoked prosocial behaviour is based upon specific feelings directed towards a concrete person and not upon some universal and field-independent moral motivation (Kantian position), although the results of studies employing questionnaire indices of empathy obviously contradict this claim.

Finally, one more perspective of studies in moral development originated from Vygotsky's approach. Within this perspective moral development is viewed as interiorization of moral standards in the course of children's social interactions and joint activities with their peers and with adults (see Bozhovitch, 1968; El'konin, 1978).

Most of the studies are highly productive and informative, both from theoretical and practical points of view (for other reviews, see Hoffman, 1988; Nucci, 1985; Onuf, 1987). Nevertheless, many problems of moral development have been studied insufficiently, the problem of the nature of moral motivation being one of them. Sometimes the problem of motivation for actual behaviour does not arise simply because only moral judgements are investigated. Sometimes an experiment or theory is described in terms of conditioning, so that the motivation concept does not seem to be necessary. As for the 'interiorization' approach, it seems to be too global and concerns the general process of motivation acquisition rather than moral motivation in its own right.

Another problem is the nature of the interrelationships between verbal and actual moral behaviours. Although this problem has been considered in many recent studies (see Eisenberg and Shell, 1986; Eisenberg and Miller, 1987) it was mainly studied by means of correlations between various scores of children's moral judgements and their moral conduct: a direct comparison of children's moral behaviour in the same 'theoretical' and 'practical' situations is still to be examined.

All this prompted me to conduct a series of studies on the development of moral behaviour and, in particular, on the motivation of children's actual behaviour in situations involving moral conflicts.

Verbal and actual moral behaviour: an experimental study

In order to compare verbal and actual moral behaviours experimentally, moral conflict situations were created that were identical in structure but different in form.

In one of these situations (it will be referred to as the 'honesty' situation) in a *first experimental condition (verbal behaviour in the imaginative experimental situation)* children were told a story about a boy who was instructed by an adult to transfer ping-pong balls from a pail into a jar using a special L-shaped shovel and without touching the balls with his hands. The boy was told that if he successfully completed the task following this rule he would receive a reward. The adult then left the room to allow the boy to work on the task unsupervised. Unable to cope with the task, the boy took advantage of the adult's absence to transfer the balls by hand. When the adult returned, the boy deceived him and received the reward promised for performing the task correctly (Subbotsky, 1983a, b). Participants were asked to judge the boy's action and to say how they would behave in the boy's place.

In the *second experimental condition (actual behaviour in the absence of direct external control)* children were placed in a situation analogous to that of the boy in the story. They were asked to transfer balls with the shovel and were promised a reward for successfully completing the task while following the rule about using the shovel and not their hands (see Figure 3.1a). After the training phase in which children could easily cope with the task because the L-shaped shovel was slightly concave, the shovel was surreptitiously replaced by an identical but slightly convex one. In the main phase of the experiment the adult left the room and observed the children's actual moral behaviour through the opening in the door.

A specific feature of this task was that it was twofold. On the one hand, it is a simple manual task (the task of transferring the balls from one vessel to another one with a special tool); as such, it contains no moral load. On the other hand, there is also moral content in the task. Before children could get access to the task they had to promise that they would not touch the balls with their hands. Now, when a concave shovel was replaced by a convex one, the task became impossible to manage. After starting the work enthusiastically (following the fast and easy execution that they experienced in the training phase), the children soon discovered that they could not do it in the right way, i.e. using the shovel only and not touching the balls with their hands. Consequently, the temptation appeared to transfer the balls with the hands. However, doing this would mean that the child broke the promise he or she had given.

This deviation, however, would make sense for the child only in one case: if he or she was going to conceal the truth and to tell the experimenter that he or she did the task in the right way (i.e. did not touch the balls with his or her hands and transferred them with the shovel). If the child did not anticipate the necessity to deceive the adult, then transferring the balls by hand did not make any sense, since the child could not hope to get the reward for the inappropriately done task (this was made clear in the instruction each child received before getting to the task: if they touched the balls with their hands they would not be given the reward).

Children's training in 'truthful behaviour' and in the ability to keep their verbal promises has been traditionally acknowledged as an

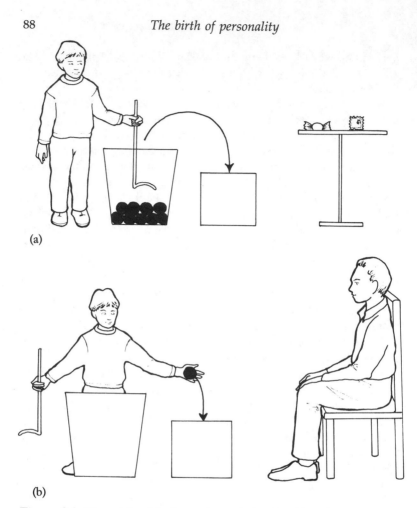

Figure 3.1 'Honesty': original experimental situation (a) and observation of the transgression (b).

important objective of moral education (Dollard, 1949). Whether this training is successful or not may be judged by special studies in which students' real cheating in examinations was found to be insignificantly related to their verbal attitudes towards cheating (Corey, 1937; Freeman and Aatov, 1960). Nevertheless, it is widely acknowledged that keeping their word is one of the most universal moral rules that people are most often challenged with in their everyday lives. This was the main reason for selecting the 'honesty' experimental situation as a model of a typical everyday moral conflict.

Of interest in this (second) condition was whether or not the children obeyed the rule, using only the special shovel and not their hands in completing the task, and whether or not they lied to the experimenter about having followed the rule. Children who followed the rule and did not lie were categorized as behaving morally.

I believe that in this experimental situation children's honest **behaviour had a moral** virtue since, first, it was *a voluntary following* of the universal moral rule ('to be honest, not to lie'), and, second, persisting in such behaviour resulted in a certain material loss to the child (the child knew that he or she would not be given a reward). The last claim, perhaps, needs clarification.

It is assumed in this book that moral behaviour is a kind of behaviour that unfolds in accordance with certain universal moral rules (such as honesty, justice, fairness, etc.).[1] However, moral behaviour has little *moral value* if it costs the subject nothing, i.e. if following moral rules brings the subject certain social or material gains or, at least, does not entail any loss. Of course, in real life much of our moral behaviour is of this type, for instance, normally we tell the truth just because it is the most easy and direct way to achieve our practical goals. However, if all situations in life were like this, then there would be no moral conflicts and no temptations to cause deviations from moral rules. Without doubt many real-life situations are not like that: basically, they challenge our sense of moral duty by promising us material or social gains if we deviate from the rules. *Only if such a temptation is overcome by a subject and if he or she has upheld moral norms at the expense of a certain loss may we talk about the moral value of moral behaviour.*[2] This type of behaviour differs from the mere following of moral rules in one important respect: whereas following these rules is often involuntary (and sometimes even unconscious) behaviour, *the true moral behaviour must be a voluntary action*, since *it is not possible to resist a temptation and overcome a conflict without being aware of the temptation, without a voluntary effort being made to overcome the conflict.*

There is no doubt that all these characteristics were present if the child kept using the shovel even when it was perfectly clear to him or her that the task could not be coped with in this way, because (1) the child knew (from the story told in the first experimental condition) about the possibility of an alternative behaviour (to transfer the balls with his or her hands and to get the reward after telling a lie to an adult), and (2) the child knew (from the adult's instruction) that if he or she did not transfer the balls he or she would not be given the reward.

However, if the child did transfer the balls with his or her hands and did deceive the adult, can we call this behaviour 'immoral'? Clearly, we can do this only if the child broke the prohibition (not to touch the balls, not to tell lie) *voluntarily*. It is obvious that if the child breaks some rules (even the moral rules) involuntarily (as happened in many experiments studying 'resistance to temptation' in children), there are no grounds for talking about moral responsibility, as we do not talk about moral responsibility in animals, infants or mentally retarded children. Fortunately, in the experimental situation in question we could easily tell the involuntary from the voluntary deviations. Namely, if the child could not resist the temptation he or she would just take the reward (a sweet, a postage stamp) and would leave the balls in the bucket, since the task of transferring the balls had nothing to do with the child's individual needs which created the temptation. However, if the child does transfer the balls using his or her hands and then lies to an adult, it is perfectly clear that the lie is a voluntary action, since *it had been planned before it had been said* (i.e. at the moment when the child was transferring the balls with his or her hands). There are, therefore, solid grounds for treating the lie as an immoral action, bearing in mind, of course, that *this immoral action is a natural stage in the development of morality and should not be identified with immoral actions in adults.*

The aim of the third experimental condition (actual behaviour in the absence of imaginary external control) was to free the child from any possible fear of punishment for the transgression or for cheating by removing the appearance of social control (i.e. the possibility of punishment) not only objectively, through the absence of the experimenter as in the second condition, but also subjectively through allowing the child to observe another child go unpunished after committing an immoral act.

The reason for this experimental procedure was that even if a child displayed moral behaviour in the second experimental condition it was still unclear whether this behaviour was motivated pragmatically or unpragmatically (i.e. intrinsically). Speaking in general terms, as far as direct external control in the second experimental condition was absent (i.e. the child was executing the task alone in the room and knew that his or her transgression would not leave any obvious traces which the adult could detect), the child's firm upholding of the rules must have been motivated unpragmatically. However, a certain doubt remains, because, despite the adult's absence, the child might still have a certain fear of control.

The fact is that most children know from their life experience that adults have superior intellectual abilities and can guess that children have offended even when there is no obvious evidence and proof of it. In order to eliminate this possible fear of the imaginative external control, the child must be assured that the adult will not investigate how the task was done and will accept the child's interpretation of events. In so far as a direct giving of such guarantees would destroy the experimental situation, they must be given indirectly, and an accurate way of doing this is to let the child to observe another child's deviation pass unpunished.

Consequently, children who behaved morally in the second condition (i.e. who neither violated the rule nor lied) were asked in the third condition to sit with another child who had broken the rules (Figure 3.1b). The latter child was asked to perform the task. The experimenter left the room for 10 minutes, secretly observing the events in the room. Upon the experimenter's return, if the model subject maintained that he or she had not broken the promise not to touch the balls (when in fact the promise had been broken), the experimenter 'believed' the child, gave him or her the promised reward, and returned the child to the classroom. After observing the 'model child' cheat and still receive a reward, the target child was asked to perform the task alone as in the second condition. Of interest here was whether or not the child continued to behave morally in the absence of imaginary external constraints (nonpragmatic morality), or if the removal of the fear of punishment would lead to cheating behaviour.

Now, if the child, after observing the other child's 'successful' deviation and cheating, still upheld the 'honesty' moral norm and did not cheat, his or her moral behaviour could obviously be viewed as motivated intrinsically. The question is, what kind of intrinsic motivation could possibly cause the behaviour? Theoretically, there can be several kinds of motives behind this behaviour, and one has no a priori criteria for making priorities. In practice, however, there are only a few reasonable hypotheses given the structure of the experiment.

Thus, for instance, the child could uphold the 'honesty' moral norm because he or she identified him/herself with the experimenter and empathized with him or her as with a person who would not like being deceived. However, first, the experimenter was a stranger to the children, and all the children knew that he or she had plenty of objects that were used as rewards (postage stamps, sweets), so that they would not do any harm to him or her if they obtained one of the objects in one or another way. Second, the moral norm itself (to be honest, not to lie) was extremely abstract: it must have been obvious to the children that violation of the norm would not immediately hurt somebody's feelings. All this makes the hypothesis of the empathically motivated moral behaviour in this situation unlikely.

Discounting this hypothesis, together with the hypothesis of the interiorized imaginative external control (see above), leaves me with only one reasonable alternative: the intrinsic motivation that could possibly force the children to abstain from deviations in the third experimental condition was their moral self-esteem, their image of themselves as of good and honest persons. It is natural to assume that deviations from the rule the children promised to uphold and subsequent deception of an adult would destroy (or, at least, damage) the children's positive moral self-esteem, and in order to avoid that, the children would uphold the 'honesty' norm even after they had observed another child's successful transgression.

A total of 136 children of mixed socioeconomic backgrounds participated in the the first two conditions of the experiment (Subbotsky, 1983b). They were all native Russian speakers and attended kindergartens in Moscow. The age of children ranged from 3 years to 6 years 11 months: they were distributed in the following age categories: from 3 years to 3 years and 11 months (38 subjects), from 4 to 4 years 11 months (39 subjects), from 5 to 5 years 11 months (31 subjects) and from 6 to 7 (28 subjects). In Condition 3 89 children participated who had revealed moral behaviour in Conditions 1 and 2; they were distributed to the same age groups with 20, 24, 19 and 18 children in each group, respectively. The results are shown in Figure 3.2.

In the first condition, almost all the children behaved similarly. That is, they censured what the boy in the story had done, confirming both that cheating was naughty and that in a similar situation they would not have broken the rules and deceived the adult. In the second condition, significantly fewer children behaved morally. While some children at all ages attempted to transfer the balls with the shovel for the entire 10-minute period as instructed without using their hands, or refused to continue the task, the remaining children transferred the balls by hand and lied to the experimenter about having complied with the rule. Age apparently had no effect on children's performance in this condition as the percentage of older and younger children who behaved immorally was basically identical (see Figure 3.2). Finally, in the third condition, focusing on nonpragmatic moral behaviour, fewer than a third of the children behaved morally. In this case, however, substantially more 6-year-old children, compared to the younger groups, adhered to the moral norms.

The results indicated that the removal of imaginary social control between Conditions 2 and 3 significantly reduced the number of children who adhered to moral norms. Thus, these data revealed age differences in children's tendencies to engage in unpragmatic moral behaviour (Condition 3) but no differences in the rate at which children engage in pragmatic moral behaviour (Condition 2). In

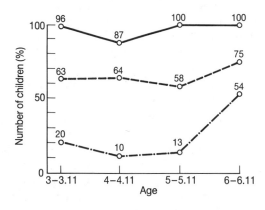

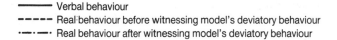

Figure 3.2 Children who observed the moral rule in the 'honesty' situation.

addition, no age differences were found in children's verbal moral behaviour. The differences between the rates of verbal moral behaviour (Condition 1) vs. real moral behaviour (Conditions 2 and 3) support our distinctions in the forms in which moral behaviour can occur. To this it can be added that the experiment described above was also conducted in Czechoslovakia with Slovak children and yielded very similar results (Pozar and Subbotsky, 1984).

One particular concern that may arise with respect to this experimental situation is that giving the reward to transgressors and no reward to the subjects who obeyed the rules might have a delayed influence upon the children's subsequent behaviour, namely, it might reinforce the transgressions and cheating, on the one hand, and facilitate a transgressive behaviour in children who did not transgress immediately after observation of the transgression. This problem contains two aspects: pragmatic and ethical.

From the pragmatic point of view the answer may be obtained empirically by simply retesting children who revealed moral behaviour in Condition 3. If observation of the successive transgression by children had some delayed effect upon their subsequent behaviour, a significant number of them would shift from upholding the rules in the immediate retest to deviating from the rules in the delayed retest. The delayed retest after a two-month interval (it will be discussed later in this chapter (see Figure 3.7, control group)) showed only an insignificant (4 to 10 per cent) reduction of moral behaviour which may well be explained by the uncontrolled external influences. This demonstrates that in those children who were able to withstand the reduction of the imaginative external control (Condition 3), moral motivation was strong enough not to be influenced by the possible delayed impact of the observation of a transgression.

From the ethical point of view, the fact of giving the promised reward to a transgressive child cannot be viewed as reinforcement of the transgression. This point seems to be important because of the possible misunderstanding of the term *reinforcement*. The misunderstanding may result from the direct transference of the term 'reinforcement' from the domain of animal psychology to the domain of education. In the domain of animal learning reinforcement is a stimulus, negative or positive, that follows immediately after a certain behavioural act and provides the act with positive or negative 'emotional meaning', or 'valency'. In other words, there is normally a direct link between the act of behaviour and the stimulus given next to it (see Figure 3.3a). Although human learning may be unfolding in a similar way (for instance, a subject may be punished or rewarded for certain types of actions in his or her attempts to get through a maze), situations like that are mostly artificial laboratory models. In real life, a subject's actions and their consequences (i.e. a teacher's mark) are mediated by a system of conscious reflections and expectations. This is especially true with respect to moral behaviour and moral transgressions such as cheating. Thus, in the situation in question ('honesty') a system of reflections mediated the link between the child's actions (transgression) and the reward he/she gets, so that the child is sure he/she gets the reward not for the transgression (transferring the balls with the help of his or her hands) and not for cheating, but for the right actions that the child invented in his or her answers to the experimenter's questions (Figure 3.3b).

The situation, therefore, involves a paradox according to which the child transgressed but is rewarded for a nontransgression. This paradox, on the one hand, makes the situation ethically acceptable for testing (since it cannot be viewed as a reinforcement of the wrongdoing) and, on the other hand, may create certain pangs of remorse in the child because of the 'cognitive clash' between what the child thinks he/she deserves (punishment) and what he/she really gets (reward). It is just this clash that may have been responsible for a

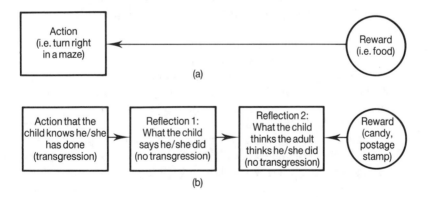

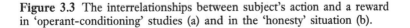

Figure 3.3 The interrelationships between subject's action and a reward in 'operant-conditioning' studies (a) and in the 'honesty' situation (b).

few cases observed in the 'honesty' situation in which children after having transgressed and cheated, refused to accept the reward (that resembles the so-called 'phenomenon of a bitter candy' described earlier by A. N. Leontiev (1977)). A similar explanation may be offered for another phenomenon which happened in approximately 80 per cent of cases after transgressions – the phenomenon of the refusal of personal contact with the experimenter. The phenomenon consisted in the children's unwillingness to stay in the experimental room after they had cheated and got the reward; even after being pressed by the experimenter to stay ('Let's read a book together', 'Let's play some games', etc.) the children were eager to leave the room under various pretexts ('I need to go to the toilet', 'I have to go, my friends are waiting for me', and so on). This behaviour was in sharp contrast to the children's behaviour in a warm-up session when all of them were eager to remain in the experimental room as long as possible, as well as to the behaviour of nontransgressive children who also never refused to stay in the experimental room for some time.

Similar results were observed in another experimental situation ('egoistic vs. prosocial'), in which children were given for their work (cutting small flags from paper) a reward – a postage stamp – which they could either keep or give to a stamp exhibition in the kindergarten (Subbotsky, 1983b). On discussing the actions of a story character who keeps the reward for himself, most of the children disapproved of his behaviour. In the real situation the child was left alone in the room with the task of cutting out some flags and going back to the classroom with or without the postage stamp (which in this case would go to the exhibition).

Here, again, the child was freed from the external control, but, in contrast to the 'honesty' situation in which direct permission to deviate from the moral rule was not possible and where liberation from the external control was achieved through sophisticated experimental procedures, in this situation the child was simply allowed to keep the reward independently of what he or she said when discussing the story character's actions. In addition, a special closed box with a split in the lid was available in which the children could put a postage stamp if they wanted to give it to the exhibition. The children, therefore, could have been sure that their donations would be anonymous, if this was what they hoped for. One more noteworthy difference between this situation and the previous one is that this one rests on an altruistic rather than on a moral norm, in the sense that conformity to altruistic norms is only desirable, whereas conformity to moral norms is considered to be obligatory.

Eighty-six children aged 4 to 4 years 11 months (13 subjects), 5 to 5.11 (24 subjects) and 6 to 7 (49 subjects) and attending kindergartens in Moscow participated as subjects. In a result, more than 90 per cent of the subjects reproduced the actions of the story character and preferred to keep the reward rather than to give it to the exhibition (see Figure 3.4).

Two other situations employed in this study ('mutual assistance' and 'justice') differed from the previous ones in that the underlying moral norms ('to help another child', 'to share one's reward with another child') were less abstract and involved the child helping a real person (a peer) who was in the same room with him or her. In the 'mutual assistance' situation in the first condition (verbal behaviour) the child heard a story about two boys, Vova and Petya, whom an adult had asked to cut flags out of paper. Vova had to cut out one flag, and Petya four. The boy who finished cutting out his flags could

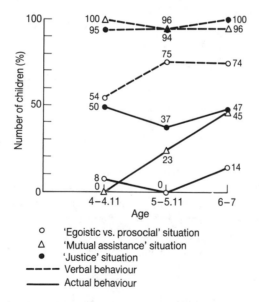

Figure 3.4 Children who observed moral rules.

either go and play with the toys near the table or to help his partner to finish his job and then they could go to play together. When Vova had finished his task, Petya asked him for help, but Vova refused and began to play. The subject was asked to say whether in his or her opinion Vova was good or bad and what the subject would do if he or she were in Vova's place. In the second condition (actual behaviour), the children were called in pairs into the room and placed in the situation portrayed in the story. Each child was faced with the possibility of coming into the advantageous position in which it was necessary to decide whether he or she would help his or her peer or immediately go on to play.

In the 'justice' situation in the first condition (verbal behaviour) the experimenter told a story about two boys, Sasha and Vitya, who were asked by an adult to cut flags out of paper. The boy who finished cutting out his flags first could receive a reward – two tokens; he could take both of them for himself, or leave one for his partner. Sasha had to cut out two flags and Vova had to cut out four. Sasha quickly finished his task and took both tokens for himself. The subject was asked to say whether Sasha was good or bad and what he or she would do in Sasha's place. In the second condition (real behaviour) children were called in pairs into the room and placed in an analogous situation. Each child had to assume the advantageous position and decide what to do with the tokens. Children of 4 to 4 years 11 months, 5 to 5.11 and 6 to 7 years of age attending kindergartens in Moscow participated as subjects: in the 'mutual assistance' situation the total number of subjects was 79 (10, 22 and 47 subjects in each age category, respectively) and in the 'justice' situation the total number of subjects was 173 (56, 52 and 65 subjects in each age category, respectively). The results are displayed in Figure 3.4.

The results (see Figures 3.2 and 3.4) showed that the development of moral behaviour with respect to various moral norms is rather uneven and displays substantial diversity. Thus, children of 4 years of age performed significantly better in their verbal behaviour in the situations 'honesty', 'mutual assistance' and 'justice' than they did in the situation 'egoistic vs. prosocial'. However, in their real behaviour 4-year-olds performed better in the 'justice' situation than in the three other situations (in the 'honesty' situation Condition 3 is used for comparison). Children of 6 years old performed equally well in their verbal behaviour in all the situations; in their real behaviour their performance was similar in all but one ('egoistic vs. prosocial') of the situations in which the developmental tendency towards better performance with age was very fragile.

However, despite all the diversity there was one phenomenon that was universal for all the situations, namely, *in all of them children from all age groups performed significantly better in their verbal behaviour than in their real behaviour.* What explanation could be offered for this phenomenon?

Obviously, in all the situations the deviations from moral norms could not be explained either by lack of knowledge about the norms or by underdevelopment of voluntary behaviour (because in all cases the majority of the children showed the ability to delay the gratification of need in order to do some work). Rather, it was the differences in *motivation* of verbal judgements and real behaviour that accounted for the prevalence of moral behaviour in children's verbal judgements and of immoral behaviour in their real actions.

As was stressed earlier (Chapter 1), verbal behaviour is normally displayed in the presence of other people (in this study – in the presence of the experimenter) and, therefore, it is under steady influence of external control. The external control creates in the child a strong motivation to conform to existing moral norms in order to get the adult's approval or to avoid reproach. As for the deviation from moral norms, verbal behaviour does not produce any significant motivation for that.

In contrast to verbal behaviour, real behaviour in two of the reported experiments ('honesty' and 'egoistic vs. prosocial') unfolded in the absence of the overt (Condition 2 for 'honesty' situation) and the imaginary (Condition 3 for 'honesty' situation) external control. In the other two situations ('mutual assistance' and 'justice') the adult's external control in the 'verbal behaviour' session was replaced by the peers' external control in the 'real behaviour' session and, therefore, became less 'salient'. Consequently, on the one hand, motivation 'to please an adult' or 'to avoid reproach' should have been weakened or eliminated. On the other hand, in order to get the reward promised a strong motivation to deviate from the moral rules appeared. This psychological factor could well be sufficient to account for the discrepancy between verbal and real behaviours in situations involving moral conflict.

But if this explanation is correct, then introducing the external control in real situations of moral conflict should prevent the deviations and bring the children's real behaviour closer to the pattern displayed in their verbal judgements. It may also be assumed that the extent to which the external control can prevent transgressive behaviour would vary with the type of controller and his or her 'emotional importance' for the child. To examine this hypothesis, the next series of experiments was conducted.

The role of peer and adult external control in children's pragmatic moral conduct

According to its definition, children's pragmatic (consequence-guided) moral conduct depends heavily on external controls. It is, therefore, of considerable importance to examine two influential sources of external control: peers and adults. In order to study these influences, children's pragmatic moral behaviour was assessed using the experimental task described above ('honesty') in the presence of either a peer who was reading a book (Condition 1) or an experimenter who was filling out forms (Condition 2) (Subbotsky, 1983b). In both instances, children were asked to transfer ping-pong balls using the special shovel without touching the balls in order to obtain a reward. Seventy-five children ranging in age from 3 to 7 years old and distributed in the age categories 3 to 3 years 11 months, 4 to 4.11, 5 to 5.11, 6 to 7 (with 21, 26, 18 and 10 subjects in each of the categories, respectively) participated as subjects. Results of this study are shown in Figure 3.5.

It is apparent from the data in Figure 3.5 that the number of children who violated the moral rule in the presence of a peer decreased significantly among 5-year-olds as compared to 3- and 4-year-olds. Moreover, 4-year-olds were more likely to try to come to an agreement with the peer than were the younger children. Finally, the number of children transgressing in the presence of a peer far exceeds the number of children transgressing in the presence of an adult regardless of the age of the child.

The results of this study illustrate age-related changes in the relative influence of peers and adults on children's pragmatic moral behaviour. First, it is obvious that the most effective factor for restraining moral transgressions is the presence of an adult. Children of all ages were more likely to engage in pragmatic moral behaviour in

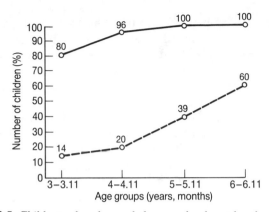

Figure 3.5 Children who observed the moral rule under the external control of a peer (---) and an adult (——).

the presence of an adult than in the presence of a peer. Peer presence failed to influence the pragmatic moral behaviour of the 3-year-olds in this study but began to have a significant impact on the rate of moral transgressions by the age of 5. Finally, older children were less likely to commit moral transgressions in the presence of either a peer or an adult than were younger children. Such differences illustrate an age-related progression in the influence of peers on children's pragmatic moral conduct.

Thus, it may be assumed from these findings that the 3-year-olds do not perceive their peers as conductors of moral rules and restrictions. However, for the 5-year-olds the peer's presence had a significantly stronger restrictive effect; they either did not violate the rule in the presence of a peer or tried to distract the peer's attention (some asked the peer to look at the bookshelves behind him or her, or to find something in the corner of the room, etc.) at the moment when they transferred the balls with their hands. Still others tried to involve the peer in a sort of agreement, suggesting that they would share their reward with the peer if he or she would not inform the adult about their offence.

Similarly, the 5-year-olds who were observing the violations behaved differently from the 3-year-olds. Whereas most of the 3-year-olds were rather indifferent to the violations, 4- and 5-year-olds either tried to stop their peer transgressing or to come to an agreement with him or her. This means that the expectations and images of both the 'acting' and 'observing the action' children change with age. On the one hand, the acting child starts to perceive the observing child as an obstacle to deviation, as a 'representative' of the external control; on the other hand, the observing child begins to feel himself or herself obliged to do something in order to either prevent or conceal the transgression.

The changes discussed may be viewed as reflecting certain changes that occur in real-life settings. It may be assumed that, as children grow older, they are not only perceived by adults as responsible for their own moral behaviour, but also as responsible for the behaviour of other children. Deliberately or not, the child is expected to take on this responsibility and to become more active in correcting and preventing the moral transgressions of other children.

In addition, as cooperative activities emerge (such as role play, joint and shared activities of all sorts, etc.) the children begin to be increasingly engaged in correcting each other's actions. This type of joint activity basically does not appear until children reach 4 or 5 years of age (see El'konin, 1960, 1978). The emergence of cooperative activities, together with the reassessment of their ability to be responsible for the moral transgressions of other children, may underlie the changes in behaviour the children display if they witness another child's moral transgression.

Consequently, the results of the study presented in this section put on the agenda the study of the views parents have about their children's ability to be responsible for their own and their peers' moral transgressions.

Parents' concepts about the age of moral responsibility

The experiments described above led me to conclude that adults' control is an important factor in children's moral development. However, the age at which adults start to perceive children as being subject to external control and the age at which children have responsibility for their actions may vary among cultures (see, for instance, Whiting and Whiting, 1975). There is no doubt that the stereotypical concepts that parents have about the development of children's consciences and their ability to adhere to moral rules will strongly influence the responses parents make to their children's moral transgressions. Bearing this in mind, I undertook another study to determine (1) the ages at which parents in Moscow consider their children to be capable of adhering to moral norms and obligations and (2) the ages at which children are thought to be responsible for controlling the moral behaviour of younger siblings (Subbotsky, 1983b).

In order to study parental conceptions of their children's moral abilities a special questionnaire was constructed. This questionnaire contained six stories about children and their behaviour in various moral conflict situations. In the first three stories the situations involved moral transgressions that were typical for young children. They were as follows:

Story 1. A strange person came around to see you in your house. Your child noticed a fountain pen in his/her pocket and, without asking for permission, took it away and started to play with it.

Story 2. Having seen an attractive toy in a small child's hands your child took it away from the child by force and began playing with it.

Story 3. You forbade your child to touch objects on your desk. In your absence the child climbed onto a chair and began to play with the items on the desk, tearing papers and breaking the inkwell.

The second set of three stories described situations in which the elder sibling failed to intervene when a younger sibling engaged in a moral transgression. They were as follows:

Story 4. You have two children: an older one and a younger one. You once noticed from the adjacent room that your younger child took a pair of scissors and started cutting the tablecloth. Your older child saw this but did not stop the younger one.

Story 5. You have three children, an older and two younger ones. In your absence one of your younger children wanted to take a toy from another one by force and when the latter resisted the former punched him/her. Your older child saw this but did not try to stop the 'aggressor'.

Story 6. You have two children, an older one and a younger one. One day you noticed from an adjacent room that in full view of the older child the younger child had thrown down and broken a porcelain vase. When you entered the room the younger child said that the vase had been broken by a neighbouring boy who came round for a while. The older child heard this but did not correct the younger one.

For both sets of stories, respondents answered two questions. First, they were asked if they considered their child guilty of a moral transgression and second they were asked if they would punish the child for misbehaviour (or the elder sibling for failing to intervene). In each instance, respondents were asked to indicate how they would respond to the behaviour of children ranging in age from 6 months to 7 years old. A total of 110 parents of 5- to 7-year-old children completed the questionnaire. The parents were Moscovites from a variety of ethnic groups and socioeconomic classes. The responses of parents to these questions are displayed in Tables 3.1 and 3.2.

Table 3.1 Percentage of parents giving confirmative answers to Stories 1–3 (%)

Question	Story	Months		Supposed age of child Years					
		6	10	1	1.5	2	3	5	7
1	1	6		27		68	91	98	100
	2		28	46		78	93	100	100
	3				44	68	90	98	98
2	1	3		7		33	60	79	87
	2		14	30		56	75	92	93
	3				35	57	84	93	95

Table 3.2 Parents giving confirmative answers to Stories 4–6 (%)

Question	Story	Supposed age of elder sibling in years				
		1.5	2	3	5	7
1	4	20	31	66	91	98
	5	14	28	61	87	93
	6			71	90	95
2	4	13	20	42	70	80
	5	10	20	35	70	80
	6			52	74	83

The results indicated that parents had different expectations for children to monitor their own and a younger sibling's moral conduct. It is apparent that by 2 years of age, parents perceive children as being responsible for their own moral transgressions and the majority report that they would punish the child for such transgressions. The parents obviously do not regard children younger than 2 years old as being conscious of, or at least responsible for, their moral transgressions, as comparatively few report that children of this age should be punished.

With regard to serving as a moral controller to a younger sibling, most parents begin to expect that children will exert some influence on younger siblings when they reach 3 years of age and the vast majority expected that older siblings would exert a strong influence on younger siblings' behaviour by the time the former group had reached the age of 5. Thus, the parents appear to expect their children to be responsible for their own and others' moral behaviour by the time they reach 5–6 years of age. These expectations should strongly influence both parental responses to their children's immoral behaviour and the type of moral behaviour (pragmatic and nonpragmatic) observed in children of different ages.

If we recall that it is just at the age of 5 that the restrictive role of peers increases significantly (see the previous section), the hypothesis about the influence of adults' expectations on the children's image of themselves as the conductors of moral requirements begins to look even more plausible than before.

Parental attitudes towards childrearing and children's moral behaviour

The studies have shown that two types of moral behaviour (pragmatic and nonpragmatic) appear in preschoolers. The question is, what kind of causes could possibly create pragmatic and nonpragmatic moral motivation in children?

With regard to pragmatic moral motivation, the causes are quite obvious: they are the development of various types of external control over children's behaviour in various moral conflict situations. As was shown above, at the age of 3 and 4 only adults' external control is strong enough to prevent a transgression, later on (at 5 and 6) peers' control gains in strength and begins to exercise a noticeable influence as a restrictive factor. Apart from direct control, various types of indirect (imaginative) control develop at the same time. As a result, pragmatic motivation of moral behaviour progressively develops at the preschool age.

It is quite clear that all sorts of external control could be allocated to the pragmatic style of social interaction – the term used in the previous chapter to refer to the way in which give-and-take in social interaction unfolds. An authoritarian style of social interaction (ASI) is one based on the unilateral external control of one party over another. In this book ASI is understood not only as overt external control: it also embraces all sorts of treatment of another person as an inferior and submissive creature whose interests are neglected or submitted to the personal interests of another individual. For instance, an egoistic action (i.e. not sharing one's reward in a situation where it is appropriate to share) is also a kind of authoritarian interaction. In contrast, a democratic style of social interaction (DSI) is a social interaction in which an adult displays unselfish behaviour by voluntarily refusing to exert control over the child unilaterally. Obviously, this style, too, can take various forms, all of which, however, have a common feature in that another individual (i.e. a child) is treated by an acting person (i.e. an adult) as an equal, or the one having the same needs and rights as the acting person.

In the previous chapter it was shown that ASI and DSI facilitate the development of either conformative (an authoritarian style) or independent (a democratic style) behaviour in preschoolers. It might also be assumed that they have another important consequence which influences the development of *two types of moral behaviour.*

Our assumption is, therefore, that *authoritarian parenting styles, in which, for example, rewards and punishments may be administered for particular behaviours, should promote the development of pragmatic morality. In contrast, the democratic parenting styles, for example, the forgiving of some mischiefs or an unconditional love for a child, should facilitate the development of nonpragmatic morality.*

Indeed, a nonpragmatic moral motivation, according to its definition, is intrinsic and does not depend upon the external control. If the child is motivated unpragmatically, he or she upholds a moral rule because of a certain inner need; for example, because of the desire to conserve his or her positive self-image, or because of empathic feelings towards the recipient of the moral action. It seems quite reasonable to suggest that it is the democratic style of social interaction in which the child's significance and importance are stressed that enhances the emergence of this intrinsic moral motivation. This hypothesis, which is merely a result of real-life observations and intuitions, also found some indirect support in experimental studies.

Thus, in an extensive study based on focused interviews, home visits and structured observations, Baumrind (1967) found that children's personal characteristics were related to the childrearing practices adopted by their parents, namely, the boys and girls who displayed most competent and mature behaviour basically had loving, demanding and understanding parents, whereas restrictive, punitive and unaffectionate parents had dysphoric and disaffiliative children. An application of Baumrind's classification of parenting patterns and types in order to assess the relationship between childrearing practices and children's moral judgements (Dunton, 1989) revealed only little relation between the two. However, in the same study parental responsiveness, psychological differentiation and demands made were reported to be positively related to the scores of children's moral reasoning (as measured by Kohlberg's scale), whereas restrictive parenting was negatively related to the maturity of children's moral judgements.

In some of the studies, self-reported parenting characteristics (such as warmth vs. coldness, restrictiveness vs. permissiveness) and children's level of moral reasoning were assessed. Hoffman and Saltzstein (1967) observed self-reported parents' discipline to be positively related to children's moral development. Hart (1988) found that fathers' self-rated involvement and affection was associated with their sons' moral development, whereas Holstein (1972) found no relation between self-reported parental warmth, control and support and children's moral judgements. However, Holstein reported that parental encouragement of their children's participation in family discussions related positively to the level of moral reasoning of the children. Similar results were reported in other studies (Parikh, 1980; Buck *et al.*, 1981).

Walker and Taylor (1991) analyzed parental interaction styles during family discussions of hypothetical and real-life moral dilemma. One of the findings was that parents' interactive style can be used to predict subsequent development of moral reasoning in children over the 2-year interval. It is noteworthy that the style that predicted the greatest moral development in children included behaviours such as 'eliciting the children's opinion, asking clarifying questions, para-phrasing, and checking for understanding' – a style that the authors associated with the 'Socratic style of questioning'. In contrast, parents' reliance on operational and informational styles was usually accompanied by a subsequent slow moral development in their children.

Viewing the studies in the context of the distinction between authoritarian and democratic styles of social interaction, one can determine certain associations between the findings and the expecta-tions of what kind of impact the styles of social interaction might have on children's moral development. Basically, the studies showed that parents' warmth, cooperation and helpfulness in treating their children (features of the democratic style of social interaction) was accompanied by children's higher actual or subsequent moral development (see Maccoby, 1980). In contrast, parents' dictatorial-ness, restrictiveness and lack of warmth and encouragement in interaction with their children (features of the authoritarian style of social interaction) was associated with relatively lower levels of maturity of children's moral reasoning. Although in the studies described only children's moral judgements were assessed, they might, nevertheless, be viewed as encouraging with regard to our hypothesis according to which children's moral behaviour can be related to their parents' styles of social interaction.

More direct evidence for this relationship was yielded in Solomon *et al.*'s study (1988). In this extended and comprehensive study the style of interaction between teachers and children was changed in order to minimize the use of extrinsic incentives and to enlarge the proportion of cooperative and helping activities, mutual responsibility and concern. The results showed that the children of the programme classrooms revealed significantly higher scores of prosocial orientation and prosocial behaviour than the children of the control classrooms – which corroborates findings showing the negative effect of external incentives on intrinsic motivation (see Lepper, 1983).

These speculations give rise to two questions regarding parenting style and moral development in children. First, what parenting styles are preferred by Moscow parents of preschoolers and young elementary school-aged children? Second, how might different parenting styles influence the development of pragmatic and nonprag-matic morality?

In order to assess these questions, we employed Varga's (1986) five-factor, non-directive questionnaire. Parents read and responded to 111 statements about children and ways of responding to children's behaviour in a variety of situations. This questionnaire allowed Varga to differentiate between four different types of parental attitudes towards children.

The first style of parental attitude is labelled *authoritarian–rejecting*. This style is characteristic of parents who ask for family counselling. Parents treat their children coldly and perceive them as naughty, nonadaptive and possessing characteristics typical of younger children (i.e. infantile values and passions are attributed to the child). This parental attitude is internally contradictory. The parents evaluate their children's abilities critically and do not believe in those capacities that are present. These parents also demand that their children achieve success in life while simultaneously punishing them severely for failure.

The second style of parental attitude is labelled *subjectively favourable*. This style of parental attitude is emotionally positive and parents exhibiting this style appear to have few difficulties in childrearing. The parents are aware of their child's individual characteristics, share the child's passions and treat the child warmly. The child's rights are respected and autonomy is granted to the child. Nevertheless, reasonable demands are placed upon children of subjectively favourable parents. Such children are encouraged to develop internal controls for education, sports, musical activities, etc. While rewards and punishments are used, they do not exceed prescribed limits.

The third style of parental attitude is labelled *symbiotic*. Children whose parents exhibit this style are loved and emotionally accepted as family members. However, symbiotic parents often appear eager to 'merge' with their children emotionally and strive to protect children from the difficulties of life. Few demands for achievement are made of the child for activities outside the family. In general, the child is treated as some kind of 'admired property' and is mildly, if ever, punished.

The fourth style of parental attitude is labelled *authoritarian–symbiotic*. Parents exhibiting this style accept their children and treat them warmly. They empathize with the child while demanding achievements in extra-familial activities. Psychological means (such as provoking anxiety or guilt) are used to control children's thoughts or deeds.

In order to study relationships between attitudes towards parenting style and children's moral development a total of 54 4–6-year-olds (27 boys, 27 girls) and their parents participated.[3] These children were selected from the larger sample of children participating in our study of children's actual moral behaviour using the criteria described below. The participants were a composite of ethnicities and socio-economic classes. All of them were Moscovites.

Children, and by extension their parents, were selected for participation in this study based on the children's actual moral behaviour in the first study presented in this chapter. Children defined as *pragmatic moralists* were those who maintained that a child should not cheat in the ball moving task when asked about a hypothetical child but did in fact cheat when they performed the task without the external control. Children classified as *nonpragmatic moralists* were children who did not cheat in the ball-moving task in the experiment under conditions free of either direct or imaginary external control. Parents of these two groups of children completed the Varga questionnaire and were classified into one of the four attitudes towards parenting style groups.

All four groups of attitudes towards parenting style were represented in the sample of parents completing the questionnaire. The authoritarian–symbiotic style (35.2 per cent of the sample) was the most common, followed by the authoritarian–rejecting and subjectively–favourable styles of attitudes towards parenting (both 22.2 per cent of the sample). The symbiotic style was the least common, although 20.4 per cent of the parents were classified as having this style.

In order to examine relationships between parental attitudes towards childrearing and children's moral behaviour, we compared the distributions across parenting styles of children whose behaviour in the moral conflict situations was pragmatic with the distributions across parenting styles of children who exhibited a nonpragmatic moral behaviour. It was expected that children who engaged in pragmatic moral behaviour would be more likely to have parents who exhibited an authoritarian–rejecting or authoritarian–symbiotic attitude towards childrearing. This relationship was expected to emerge because of the heavy emphasis on punishment and reward (either real or psychological) exhibited in the attitudes of such parents. In contrast, children from both subjectively–favourable and symbiotic families were expected to be found primarily in the nonpragmatic group as a result of their parents' tendencies to employ parenting techniques that encourage the initiative and stress the equality and mutual trust in social interactions between adults and children.

The results (see Table 3.3) supported the majority of these hypotheses. Children from authoritarian–rejecting families were significantly ($p < 0.05$) more likely to be classified as pragmatically than nonpragmatically moral. Moreover, the majority of pragmatically oriented children came from families in which the parenting style was classified as either authoritarian–rejecting or authoritarian–symbiotic. In contrast, nonpragmatically oriented children were more likely to be from subjectively–favourable or symbiotic families. As for the children from authoritarian-symbiotic parents, they appeared equally likely to be classified as pragmatic or nonpragmatic in their moral behaviour. This result may reflect the fact that authoritarian–symbiotic parents are strict in their enforcement of moral behaviour but instil internalized (psychological) controls over their children's behaviour.

The data are in concordance with our predictions regarding relationships between style of social interaction (as exemplified in parental attitudes towards childrearing) and the development of moral behaviour. It appears evident that the authoritarian-rejecting parenting style is based largely on behaviours encompassed by the authoritarian social interaction style. In contrast, the subjectively favourable and symbiotic parenting styles appear best captured by the democratic social interaction style. These differences may explain the differential distribution of morally pragmatically and nonpragmatically oriented children among these three parental attitude groups. The

Table 3.3 Pragmatic vs. nonpragmatic children in families with a particular parental attitude type

Parental attitude type	Type of child behaviour	
	Pragmatic	Nonpragmatic
1. Authoritarian-rejecting	9	3
2. Subjectively-favorable	3	9
3. Symbiotic	3	8
4. Authoritarian-symbiotic	9	10
Total	24	30

authoritarian–symbiotic parenting style is likely to include elements of both the DSI and ASI styles, which may account for the fact that children from families exhibiting this style of parenting were equally distributed among pragmatic and nonpragmatic moralists. This parenting style may promote either a pragmatic or a nonpragmatic moral development.

The findings are obviously in favour of the *hypothesis about the positive relationships between the democratic style of social interaction adopted by adults in their communication with children and children's moral behaviour.* Nevertheless, the results are only correlational and, therefore, indirect. In order to check whether the relationship claimed in the hypothesis is *causal*, the intervention study was needed.

Influence of the positive and negative experience of social interaction on children's subsequent moral behaviour

One of the examples of authoritarian or democratic styles of social interaction is that in which a person experiences another person's egoistic or altruistic (moral) treatment of him or her. Indeed, experiencing another person's moral and respectful treatment can enhance moral self-esteem in a child and encourage the child 'to respond' in the same moral way in his or her subsequent behaviour; by the same token, if a child comes across a person who treats him or her unfairly, this may prompt the child to follow this mode of treatment when an opportunity for this occurs and even view this unfair behaviour as a sort of 'compensation' for the damage suffered before.

Some experimental evidence in favour of this hypothesis can be found in studies of 'reciprocity' (Berkowitz and Daniels, 1964; Greenglass, 1969; Harris, 1970). Basically, it was shown in these studies that subjects who had become recipients of altruistic acts tended to show more altruism in their subsequent behaviour than those who experienced egoistic behaviour by their partners. However, the studies cannot give a direct answer to the problem we deal with in this section since, first, they were conducted with adults and older children, and, second, an adult (not a peer) model was used in the child study (Harris, 1970) who both shared her reward with children and was a recipient of the children's sharing in a subsequent experiment.

The problem of the study was, therefore, to determine whether the child's experiencing of an altruistic (egoistic) act by a peer enhances the tendency in him or her to act in an altruistic (egoistic) way relative to a different peer. Children's behaviour in the 'justice' situation was studied. In the first session ('no prior experience') the procedure was the same as described above in this chapter (real behaviour). Two children were asked to do unequal portions of work for which they were promised two tokens. The winner could either keep both of them or take only one and leave the other for the partner. The children who were given a smaller job in this session and, therefore, were put in a favourable position, composed the control group of subjects. The children who were given larger portions of work and could not win the 'competition' were later divided into two experimental groups: those who experienced altruistic behaviour by a peer (i.e. who were shared the tokens with – group 1) and those who experienced egoistic behaviour of a peer (group 2).

In the second session ('negative vs. positive prior experience') only children of the experimental groups participated. They were given the same task as before; this time, however, they were put in the favourable position and, therefore, faced with the moral challenge. In order to prevent their decisions being influenced by a possible desire to reciprocate, their partners were replaced by other peers. It was assumed that the results of this session would give the answer to the major question, namely, whether the children who experienced a partner's altruistic behaviour in the first session would behave in a similar way in this session, and vice versa. *If this were the case, there would be more sharing children in group 1 and more nonsharing children in group 2 than in the control group.*

Children attending kindergartens in Moscow participated as subjects in the first session (56 4-year-olds, 52 5-year-olds and 65 6-year-olds). In the second session numbers of children in the control group, group 1 and group 2 were as follows: 26, 13 and 17 among 4-year-olds, 24, 14 and 14 among 5-year-olds and 32, 12 and 21 among 6-year-olds. The results (Figure 3.6) showed that in 4- and 5-year-old children the numbers of subjects who reproduced altruistic or egoistic modes of behaviour in the second session did not differ significantly from the numbers of control children revealing the same modes of behaviour. In 6-year-olds, however, significantly more

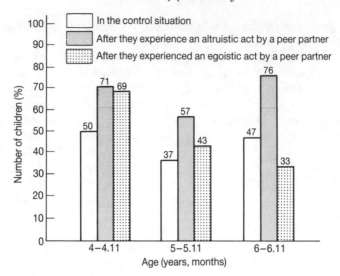

Figure 3.6 Children who shared their rewards.

($p < 0.05$) children shared their reward with a peer among the children who had positive prior experience than among the children of the control group, although the behaviour of children who had negative prior experience did not substantially differ from control children's behaviour.

The results partially support the hypothesis that a child's experience of another person's positive moral action enhances his or her own moral (altruistic) behaviour. This progress cannot be explained merely by the children's desire to reciprocate, since the recipients of their altruistic acts in the second experimental session and the children who caused positive prior experience in the first experimental session were not the same.

However, the results are limited in many respects. First, the influence of positive prior experience was only revealed in 6-year-old children and not in 4- and 5-year-olds. Second, the influence of negative experience was revealed in neither of the age groups. This relatively weak influence of positive prior experience and the absence of the influence of negative prior experience can be explained by their situational character; it may well be assumed that the results would be more impressive if this experience was stronger and longer. However, even if this was the case, the interpretation of exactly what caused the change in the behaviour of children who did have positive or negative prior experience would still be difficult since in the 'justice' situation children not only experience another person's moral or egoistic actions but they also witness positive or negative models at the same time. It is not clear, for instance, whether it was the experience of DSI alone that caused the improvement in 6-year-olds' subsequent altruistic behaviour, or if the improvement was the combined effect of the experience and observation of a positive model. Finally, the 'justice' experimental situation involves a permanent external control over children's behaviour and therefore does not allow any conclusions to be drawn with respect to the quality of the moral behaviour that emerges. It remained unclear whether the children's sharing behaviour was of a pragmatic or unpragmatic nature. In order to separate the role of model from the role of experiencing the DSI, as well as in order to determine the influence of various forms of the DSI on the development of unpragmatic moral behaviour in children of various ages, the following series of experiments was conducted.

Enhancing moral behaviour in a classroom: intervention studies

The task for the intervention studies was, therefore, to create conditions that would or would not implicate the elements of the democratic style of interaction and to determine the effect of the conditions on children's behaviour in experimental situations involving moral conflicts. It may be assumed that under the conditions that implicate DSI elements the number of children capable of displaying nonpragmatic moral behaviour will significantly increase, whereas in the conditions involving no such elements the increase in the number of nonpragmatically oriented children cannot be expected.

In practice, there are several indirect ways of furthering moral education. These methods have been formulated over time, encouraged by a growing awareness that there is a demonstrable correlation between the use of those methods and the growth of moral character, goodness, altruism and other such qualities in the child.

The first of these methods is *the method of influence by personal example*. The favourable effect of a positive moral example has been documented since Plato's days. Thus, in his *Grundlegung zur*

Metaphysik der Sitten (Foundations of the metaphysics of morals), Kant wrote:

> The most ordinary observation reveals that if we are presented with an honourable act . . . [performed] with no intention of deriving therefrom any advantage whatsoever . . . the greatest trials and temptations notwithstanding, that act far surpasses and eclipses any comparable act that has been influenced, albeit to the slightest degree, by some alien motive [towards personal advantage – E.S.]; it elevates the spirit and evokes the desire to act likewise. Even young people feel that influence, and their duties therefore should never be presented to them in any way but this. (Kant, 1965b, p.248)

In contemporary psychology this method is applied in various kinds of 'learning through observation'. Basically, the studies showed a significant influence by a positive model on subjects' subsequent prosocial behaviour (see Wagner and Wheeler, 1969; Harris and Samerott, 1975).

The second method could be referred to as *the method of generating a sense of guilt*. It has been noticed that a person is inclined to perform unselfish acts when suffering from guilt because of some recent unpunished transgression. This cause-and-effect serves as the basic thrust in many works of fiction, and also underpins the concept of morality in psychoanalysis. In recent years there have been attempts to subject this factor to empirical verification, in the light of psycho-analytical studies of altruism (Freedman and Wallington, 1967; Wallace and Sadalla, 1966).

The third method is widely known as *inducting the child into adult activity*. Educational practice has established that children are more inclined to obey rules and adhere to norms unselfishly if they are induced into adult activity and accorded a social position as similar as possible to that of an adult. This induction is an organic aspect of childhood in many non-European cultures (see, for instance, Mead, 1963). In European cultures, it is seen rather as a psychotechnical contrivance, which was applied, for example, in Soviet education by Makarenko and others of his school (see Bordichenko, 1965; Borishevsky, 1965).

Finally, the fourth method may be called *a method of satisfying basic needs*. It had been noted that, in general, a person is more inclined to perform moral and unselfish acts when his or her basic needs are maximally satisfied. The satisfaction of the need for social interaction is of particular importance here. It is common knowledge that warm emotional relations within the family promote a child's moral development, and that coldness, rejection, and an authoritarian approach make selfishness flourish.

Each of these four methods is double-edged. On the one hand, they can all serve as a 'veiled' means of intensifying social controls (by reward and punishment): a positive example, for instance, can be presented in such a way as to instil in the child a fear of transgressing. In such a case the use of these methods helps shape pragmatic moral behaviour. On the other hand, some of these methods can become a catalyst for nonpragmatic moral actions.

Indeed, at least three of the methods mentioned may include elements of the DSI. With respect to 'engaging the child in adults' activity' and 'satisfying basic needs' it seems to be quite obvious since both of them include elements of trust and 'equality' on the part of the adult that may have a certain impact on the emergence of a positive 'moral self-image' in a child. The presence of DSI elements in the 'induction of a sense of guilt' is less obvious; nevertheless, this presence becomes more obvious if it is taken into account that the sense of guilt invoked in a child by a certain misdeed may be accompanied by a forgiving of the misdeed by the adult. If this is the case, such forgiving alone may well be perceived by the child as a sign of trust and benevolence and thus encourage his or her positive moral self-image.

Hence, the first stage of the interventional work (Experiment 1) was aimed at assessing these four educational methods as means of catalysing a nonpragmatic moral behaviour. Five experimental conditions were devised, using as subjects children who had violated moral norms in the pretests in 'honesty' moral conflict situations (see Subbotsky, 1979a, 1983b).

The *first condition* investigated the influence of a positive age–peer example. A 'rule-breaker' was simply asked to sit in the room; a child who had obeyed the rules was asked to perform the task (of transferring the balls with a shovel). The experimenter left the room and observed the conduct of these two children for 10 minutes. On his or her return, the experimenter sent the 'model subject' back to his or her room and asked the 'observer' to perform the task alone (posttest).

The *second condition* was identical to the first except that the positive role model was not a peer, but an adult.

The *third condition* was aimed to study the effect of guilt and forgiving. The child was called into the room and left there to play with an electric cross-country vehicle whose battery contacts had previously been loosened. The experimenter 'discovered' the damage, looked pained about it but then said that he or she 'forgave' the child and would buy another vehicle. After that the experimenter asked the child to perform the posttest (which was the same in all the experimental conditions and identical with the pretest).

In the *fourth condition* the effect of including the child into an adult role was explored. The experimenter expressed his or her trust in the subject and requested his or her help. He or she asked the child to teach the younger one how to perform the task and to advise him or her that all the rules should be observed. Then the same subject was asked to monitor the actions of the child of his or her own age in the performance of the same task. This latter child had already broken the rules; the subject was thus put into a situation of conflict with his or her peer. The posttest was performed at the end.

The aim of the *fifth condition* was to ascertain the effect that satisfaction of the child's need for emotionally positive interaction with adults had on the tendency to perform a moral action. Over the course of two months, the subjects were regularly assembled for sessions, during which the experimenter played with them, read to them, told them stories and chatted with them on topics of personal interest. When emotionally positive relations had been established with these children, each became the subject of two posttests: in the first, the instructions on the 'honesty' task were given by the experimenter (*a*), and in the second, by an adult stranger (*b*).

The *control group* consisted of rule-breakers who had not been exposed to any of these methods: the posttests with this group were conducted two months after the conclusion of the five-phase experiment described above, in order to measure any spontaneous change in the children's disposition to perform a moral act.

Children of two age groups (younger – 210 children from 3 to 5 years of age, and older – 220 children from 5 to 7 years of age) participated as subjects. The results (see Figure 3.7) indicated that – as opposed to the result of studies of children's altruistic behaviour (Bryan and Walbek, 1970a, b; Bryan, 1971) – a positive example did not have a substantial effect on the children's moral conduct in a situation involving free choice. The generation of a sense of guilt and forgiving, induction into an adult position and emotionally positive

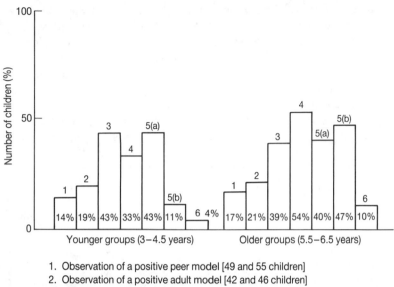

1. Observation of a positive peer model [49 and 55 children]
2. Observation of a positive adult model [42 and 46 children]
3. Forgiving of guilt [34 and 36 children]
4. Being in the role of a moral educator [15 and 35 children]
5. Extended emotionally positive communication [45 and 28 children]
   (a) test is given by the experimenter
   (b) test is given by a stranger
6. Control [25 and 20 children]

Figure 3.7 Children who revealed moral behaviour in posttests ('honesty') in various conditions (1–6). (Total numbers of younger and older subjects are shown in brackets.)

interaction significantly increased the number of children who performed a moral action.

With respect to the success of the last three conditions, an alternative interpretation may be put forward which attributes this success to the children's belief that they would be rewarded eventually even if they did not complete the task set. This objection, however, does not take into account that the children had already performed the control task in the pretest and got the reward after violating the rule. They knew, therefore, that violation would be the quickest way to obtain the reward and that the experimenter would not try to find out how they had accomplished the task. In addition to this, in the posttest, as in the pretest, all the children were warned before the experiment that they would be given the reward only if they managed to transfer the balls in the right way – with the shovel and without touching the balls with their hands – and if they did not they would not be given the reward. The combination of the children's transgressive past experience and the instruction given makes the interpretation of the positive results through 'the hope for the subsequent reward' very unlikely.

One can see, however, that the improvement thus achieved did not exceed 30–50 per cent of the original number of subjects. It may be assumed that if these psychotechnical methods are comprehensively applied, there might be a certain rise in facilitating effect. It would seem that including the child into an adult position and establishing emotionally positive interaction between adult and child are the least understood and most promising of the four methods. Nevertheless, it is important to stress that these methods do not have unlimited potential: no previous influence can guarantee determining a child's conduct precisely because he or she is free when he or she performs a moral action. Yet the experiments described here did point to evidence of a spontaneous kinesis from pragmatic to nonpragmatic moral actions, and vice versa.

The discrepancy between the results of the first condition of this study and the studies of children's altruistic behaviour (Bryan and Walbek, 1970a, b) in which a significant influence of a positive model on children's subsequent prosocial behaviour was shown, can be, at least in part, accounted for by the differences in the 'prosocial norms' used in the studies. Whereas in the studies of children's altruistic behaviour a 'norm of donation' was used most often which appeals directly to children's emotions and whose violation causes an obvious damage to other children, in this study the 'honesty' norm was used, which is quite abstract and can hardly evoke compassionate feelings of any kind in children.

In order to bring the experiment closer to the experimental model used in the studies of altruism, Experiment 2 was carried out. In this experiment the experimental situation 'egoistic vs. prosocial' (see the second section of this chapter) was taken as pre- and posttests, whereas for the enhancing influences three of the four above described methods (the method of a positive model – the first experimental condition; the method of generating a sense of guilt – the second experimental condition; and the method of inducting the child into the controller's social position – the third experimental condition) were employed (Subbotsky, 1979b). Sixty children aged from 6 to 7 years old (20 in each experimental condition) who kept the postage stamp in the pretests took part as subjects in the experiment. An adult female (one of the kindergarten's teachers) figured as a model in the experiment.

The results were similar to the results of Experiment 1. Whereas in the second and third experimental conditions the numbers of children who gave the postage stamps for the exhibition were significant in posttests (30 per cent and 50 per cent of children in each of the conditions, respectively), the demonstration of a positive model had no effect on children's altruistic behaviour. Although the results again were at odds with the Bryan and Walbek's study, they cannot be viewed as contrasting; the present study was not a replication and certain important differences in methodologies employed (the type of reward, the way of sharing, etc.) may still account for the discrepancy.

However, the results of Experiment 2 are in concordance with Experiment 1 in which the 'honesty' norm was employed in pre- and posttests. They showed that between the 'demonstration of a positive model' method and the other methods employed certain important differences may exist. It can be assumed, for instance, that the 'demonstration of a positive model' method, being a unilateral suggestive influence upon a child, stands closer to the authoritarian style of social interaction, whereas the other three methods involved bilateral communication between children and adults and approached the democratic style of social interaction. If this is true, it may well account for the differences in efficiency of these two types of methods as enhancers of children's moral and altruistic behaviour.

Enhancing moral behaviour in preschoolers in an extensive classroom experiment

The next step in the intervention studies (Experiment 3) was the organization of a comprehensive and sufficiently prolonged development of moral behaviour in children in a kindergarten classroom setting (Subbotsky, 1981b, 1983b). I assumed that this development would result in a substantial increase in the number of children observing moral norms of behaviour.

Due to the complexity of the problem there has been very little research on enhancing moral and social values in children in a classroom. Those studies that are available seem to show that a friendly and emotionally positive atmosphere in a classroom does enhance cooperative and moral values. Among the factors enhancing positive intergroup interactions in students, teachers' warmth and acceptance towards the children (Serow and Solomon, 1979) and teachers' combined emphasis on their students' academic success and interpersonal relations (Prawat and Nickerson, 1985) were pointed out. The above mentioned study by Solomon *et al.* (1988) presented results of the five-year programme designed to enhance prosocial development in elementary school children. In this study, stress was made in the programme classrooms on encouraging such activities as cooperative activities in small groups, activities promoting social understanding through teacher-directed discussions of events that arise spontaneously in a class, and also on the teacher's highlighting of prosocial values and behaviours in a classroom and on 'helping activities' among students. The last component, which included encouraging children to help other students, to participate in tutoring, in school improvement and community service activities and in classroom chores, is of a special interest for us since it is very similar to the type of intervention employed in the study presented in this chapter. The results of Solomon *et al.*'s study indicated that students in programme schools scored significantly higher on such indices of interpersonal behaviours as 'supportive and friendly behaviours' and 'spontaneous prosocial behaviours' than did children from comparison schools. However, the complex and comprehensive character of the intervention strategies employed in Solomon *et al.*'s study makes it difficult to determine the differential effect of each separate strategy in enhancing children's prosocial behaviour.

In the study presented here, the pre- and posttests were, in general, analogous to one another and included a study of the children's behaviour in five situations of moral conflict that had been tested in earlier studies (Subbotsky, 1978a, b). Each situation had two variations: a verbal one and a real one. First, the child was told a story whose hero (also a preschool child) had faced a situation of moral conflict and had broken a moral norm. The child was asked to repeat the story, assess the hero's acts, and say how he or she would have acted in his place. In this way it was determined whether the child knew the particular norm and whether he or she considered its fulfilment binding on him/herself. Then the child was placed in a real situation wholly analogous to that depicted in the story; the child's behaviour in this situation was compared with his or her verbal behaviour.

The *first three test situations* ('honesty', 'egoistic vs. prosocial' and 'mutual assistance') were described earlier in this chapter.

In the *fourth situation* ('justice 1'), in the first variation the children were told a story about two boys, Vasya and Kolya, whom an adult asked to divide up four toys between themselves, two large nice ones and two small poor ones. Vasya took the large nice toys for himself, and Kolya was left with the small poor ones. In the second variation the child was called into the experimental room and asked to divide up four toys (two good and two bad) between him or her and his or her partner, the experimenter emphasizing especially that the child could take any toys he or she wished, even all of them.

The *fifth situation* (called 'justice 2' in this study) was identical to that described earlier in this chapter under the name 'justice'.

The training that took place in the period between the pretests and the posttests, was of a complex nature and included three forms of work with the children in the experimental group. All three forms aimed at imparting the functions of a champion and defender of behaviourial norms: the organization of childcare, 'gift-giving days' and experimental-formative influences.

At the very beginning of the *first training procedure (caring for younger children)* a solemn ritual of accepting the children into the experimental group as 'teacher's helpers' was carried out. From this time on, at least once a day a small group of teacher's helpers (four or five children) were to pin on their badges and special red ribbons and go off to the supervised group of smaller children. The helpers assisted the younger children in dressing themselves for a walk, in undressing after the walk and tidying up their scattered toys. The teacher in the small group made sure that each child had a helper. The principle of voluntariness was strictly observed in choosing the group of helpers.

It was assumed that participation in this helping work would aid the children in assuming the position of a champion and defender of norms, would develop in them an attitude toward themselves as older children and thus would help to inculcate a nonpragmatic positive self-image in them.

During the *second training procedure ('gift-giving days')*, once or twice a week before a modelling, poster making, or drawing session, the teacher would say to the children: 'What shall we give the little children today? Let's give them (and he or she would name the content of the session).' After carrying out the task, the children took their drawings or models and went into the auditorium, where, under solemn conditions, with musical accompaniment, each child gave his or her present to one of the smaller children in the supervised group.

The *third training procedure ('experimental-formative influences')* was exercised in the three situations used in the test experiments: 'honesty', 'egoistic vs. prosocial' and 'mutual assistance'. In the 'honesty' situation, the experimenter called a teacher's helper into the room and said to him or her: 'You did the job of shifting the balls with the shovel well and did so honestly. But there are children who used their hands and cheated. Help me to teach these children to do the task correctly – OK?' If the child agreed, the experimenter called a child from another group who had been inclined to break the rule and asked him or her to do the task while the teacher's helper saw to it that no rules were broken in the process. The adult went out of the room and observed the behaviour of the children for five minutes through a screen.

In the 'egoistic vs. prosocial' situation, the experimenter asked the teacher's helper to look after a smaller child inclined to selfish acts and counsel him or her to give the token to the exhibition. The helper child was told not to force the child, but only attempt to persuade him or her to perform a prosocial act.

In the 'mutual assistance' situation, the helper was asked to see that children from the other kindergarten group behaved correctly in the situation; if one of the partners immediately went over to the toys after finishing cutting out his or her flags, the helper was supposed to indicate to him or her the need to help his or her 'friend'.

The essence of the experimental-formative influences was, of course, not to force the 'offenders' to 'moralize' before other children, but to show trust in them. By asking a child to assume the position of a helper, the experimenter raised him or her to the level of an adult and expressed faith in that child's moral capacities, encouraging him or her to evaluate him/herself anew. This trust (like any social encouragement), expressed in the response to the immoral act of the child, was supposed to be a particular form of the democratic style of social interaction. It was assumed (and this has been confirmed in my previous experiments) that by showing trust in a child we helped to cultivate positive moral self-esteem (regarding oneself as a good person) and thus to foster nonpragmatic moral behaviour.

In the 'justice 1' and 'justice 2' situations, the experimental-formative influence was not applied. This was for the purpose of distinguishing the pure effect of these influences from the effect of upbringing in general: if in the control experiments in these situations an improvement took place in the behaviour of the experimental group, it would mean that the effect of all the techniques of upbringing and education (caring for smaller children, the gift-giving days and the experimental-formative influences in the other situations) was generalized; if, on the other hand, an improvement took place only in the 'honesty', 'egoistic vs. prosocial' and 'mutual assistance' situations, it would mean that only the experimental-formative influences were an effective means of education.

For the experimental group we chose 30 children, aged 4 to 5 years, from a kindergarten in Moscow. We selected children of this age for two reasons; first, many of them still required the cultivation of moral behaviour; and second, they were capable (in contrast to 3-year-olds) of fulfilling the functions of teacher's helpers. The control group (30 children) was an analogous group from another Moscow kindergarten. The pre- and posttests were carried out in October 1979 and March 1980, respectively. The training lasted four-and-a-half months. In addition to the author, a group of students from the Department of Psychology of Moscow State University and kindergarten teachers took part in the training of these children.

All the children save one agreed enthusiastically to help to take care of younger children and never refused to go to their charges during the whole session. All the caretakers did their job well and created a positive emotional background. Some children even complained that they were not asked to do the job often enough. Within a month each 'tutor' already knew his or her responsibilities well; he or she was able to find his/her charge quickly and help the young child with dressing or undressing and putting clothes away. Not one case of unfriendliness or unkindness by the caregivers to their young charges was observed. The children who were normally lively and boisterous in the classroom became more serious and calm while performing their duties, and only a few caregivers sometimes shifted from performing their duties to playing with the young children. Upon returning to their own group, the 'tutors' would tell their friends what they had done with the younger children ('It's a shame that we can't help feed the little ones, but there is not enough time.'). The 'tutors' were particularly happy to meet the younger children after a two-week interruption because of illness; they dressed their wards, dressed themselves and asked teachers to allow them to play with the younger ones in the playground.

During the gift-giving days the children revealed an obvious desire to give their clay figures or drawings to the younger children. Sometimes during their regular lessons the children did their tasks slowly and without enthusiasm, then on the 'giving days' their behaviour changed drastically and they did their best, accompanying their work with comments such as 'And I am going to give this as a present', 'I'm going to do my best to draw for the young children because they can't draw for themselves', 'I'm going to make such a nice drawing that all the young children would like it', etc. The very act of gift-giving was performed in a positive emotional background: most of the children smiled at the young ones and were anxious that they should like their presents. After the giving act each tutor saw his or her charge back to the classroom. On average each caregiver participated in the gift-giving days 21 times.

In the experimental-formative influences *only those children who had broken moral rules in the pretests participated.* According to the results, they could be divided into three groups. Children of the first group were delighted by the experimenter's request to help and actively assumed the position of defender of moral norms. They watched the behaviour of the acting child attentively and reminded him or her that the rules should be strictly observed. Here are some abstracts from the recorded results:

'Honesty' situation: Ira P. (a girl, 4 years 6 months) observes the activity of another girl, Marina M. (5.3). As soon as the experimenter went out, Marina knocked the ball onto the floor with the shovel. Ira picked up the ball and put it back in the bucket. Marina, holding the ball on the shovel with her hand, placed it in the can. Ira said to her: 'You can't hold it with your hands.' Marina worked with the shovel for a short time, and again tried to break the rule, but encountered Ira's resistance. Marina returned the balls to the bucket and for the rest of the time tried to get them out with the shovel.

'Egoistic vs. prosocial' situation: Natasha D. (a girl, 4.7) observes the activity of Tanya M. (a girl, 3.4). Tanya cut out the flags, and the two girls remained quietly busy. When Tanya had trouble, Natasha showed her how she could hold the scissors better. Tanya took the token and prepared to go out; Natasha said to her: 'It's better if you put it in the box for the exhibition.' Tanya called to the experimenter: 'But I want to keep the token for myself.' She went out with the token.

'Mutual assistance' situation: Egor B. (a boy, 4.5) observed the activity of Ira K. (a girl, 3.6) and Elik M. (a boy, 3.4). Elik quickly cut out his flags and immediately ran over to the toys. Egor went up to him: 'Wait, your friend needs some help.' Elik returned and helped Ira finish her work.

Children of the second group, too, accepted the experimenter's request enthusiastically and promised to help, but finding themselves alone with the acting child they abandoned their promises, watched the child's transgressions with indifference and did not tell the experimenter about them. The children of the third group promised the experimenter to help but in reality taught the acting child how to break the rules and to deceive the experimenter. The last two groups were formed of children who refused to assume the role of champion and defender of moral norms. Here is an example.

'Honesty' situation: Ilya T. (a boy, 4 years 7 months) volunteered to help the experimenter, and for a long time insisted that he be picked. The experimenter left him alone with Dima K. (a boy, 4.3). For some time Ilya observed with curiosity Dima's unsuccessful attempts to shift the balls with the shovel, then he said to him: 'But you can do it with your hands' and helped the offender. He looked stealthily towards the door and said to Dima: 'Tell them that you did it with the shovel. Don't say that you did it with your hands.' Then he went up to the door and knocked; the experimenter came in. Ilya: 'Dima's finished already.' The experimenter said: 'Dima, did you do it with the shovel or touched the balls with your hands?' Dima said: 'With the shovel.' Dima went out. The experimenter asked Ilya: 'Did he tell the truth?' Ilya smiled craftily and said: 'Yes, he didn't break the rules.'

In sum, the average numbers of experimental-formative influences per child were: in the 'honesty' situation – 15, in the 'egoistic vs. prosocial' situation – 6, and in the 'mutual assistance' situation – 5.

A comparison of the results of the pretests and posttests in the 'honesty' (numbers of children tested were 24 in the experimental group and 20 in the control group), 'egoistic vs. prosocial' (numbers of children were 23 and 23, respectively), and 'mutual assistance' (numbers of children were 21 and 14, respectively) situations are shown in Figure 3.8.

As the figure shows, there was no notable increase in the number of children fulfilling the norms in the experimental groups; it remained at approximately the same level. In the control group, the number of children fulfilling the norms for 'honesty' and 'mutual assistance' decreased substantially. Presumably, this decrement may be due to the fact that in the pretests children of the control group scored unusually highly on the 'honesty' and 'mutual assistance' tasks and significantly higher than children of the experimental group. Although we did not make a special search to determine the causes of this difference, it may well have been a result of the individual teaching style of the teacher who was in charge of the control classroom prior to the commencement of the experiment. Since kindergarten teachers change quite often and in most cases there is no possibility for experimenters to influence this process in control classrooms, it may have happened that in the middle of the experimental programme the control class had a new teacher who made less emphasis on mutual assistance and moral values than did

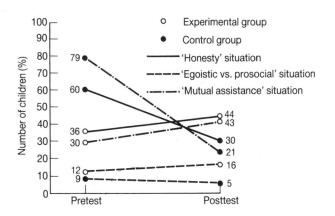

Figure 3.8 Children who observed the moral norms in pretest and posttests.

the previous one; as a result, the numbers of children who conformed to the moral norms in the 'honesty' and 'mutual assistance' tasks simply dropped closer to the average for children of this age.

As our earlier data had demonstrated, during the repeats of the testing procedures a spontaneous dynamic was observed in the children's behaviour. Some of those who in the first test had observed the norms, in the second test, two or three months later, violated them, and vice versa. It may be assumed that the reason for this dynamic pattern was that the child talked with his or her playmates and adults outside the laboratory, so that in some children the moral motives were reinforced, whereas in others they were weakened. The influence of this 'life-context' impelled me to look at the results in a more differentiated way in order to discern the internal dynamic that took place during the experiment in both groups. The results are shown in Figure 3.9.

Figure 3.9 shows that, although the outward behaviour of the

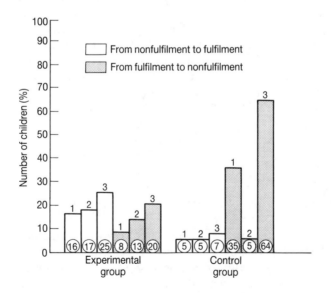

Figure 3.9 Children altering their behaviour in the posttests compared to the pretests in the 'honesty' situation (1), the 'egoistic vs. prosocial' situation (2) and the 'mutual assistance' situation (3).

children in the experimental group remained the same, there was a considerable internal dynamic that remained concealed: some of the children who in the pretests fulfilled the norm, violated them (negative dynamic in the control experiments), but in others the opposite tendency was observed (positive dynamic). We also see that in the experimental group a considerable positive dynamic was observed in all three situations (the change was significant), whereas in the control group it was negligible. The negative dynamic was considerable in both groups.

To determine the dependence of the internal dynamic of the children's behaviour on two factors, namely, participation in the experimental-formative influences and assumption of the position of champion and defender of the norm, Table 3.4 was compiled. In this table in the last two columns a percentage of children is shown who passed either from immoral to moral behaviour or vice versa in the posttests compared with the pretests. Since those children who upheld moral norms in the pretests were not subjected to the experimental-formative influences, and of those who were subjected not all accepted the position of 'defender of the norms', the dynamics of moral behaviour (in pretests as compared to the posttests) was analyzed separately for these three subgroups of subjects. For various reasons (illness, absence, etc.) not all of the children could participate in the posttests, and the numbers of children in the subgroups are given separately. The percentage is calculated relative to the subgroups of children that are shown in the first two columns, so that, for instance, the first line shows that out of seven children who transgressed in the pretests and assumed the position of defender of the norms in the 'honesty' situation 57 per cent shifted from nonfulfilment in the pretest to fulfilment in the posttest, and the remaining 43 per cent retained their transgressive behaviour; the third line shows that out of nine children who did not transgress in the pretests 22 per cent demonstrated transgressive behaviour in the posttests and the rest retained their moral behaviour, etc. (a dash means that this part of the column is irrelevant to the line).

The table shows that a positive dynamic took place only in children who had actively assumed the position of champion and defender of the norms in the experimental-formative influences; the children who did not assume the position retained their transgressive behaviour in posttests, and there was a negative dynamic in children who did not participate in the formative-influences sessions. The results of the

Table 3.4 Quantitative parameters for the dynamics of behaviour of children in the experimental group as a consequence of experimental-formative influences and the child's assuming the position of champion and defender of norms

Situation	Number of children in the subgroup	Subgroup	Number of children passing from nonfulfilment to fulfilment of norms (%)	Number of children passing from fulfilment to nonfulfilment (%)
'Honesty'	7	Children assuming the position	57	—
	7	Children not assuming the position	0	—
	9	Children not subjected to the experimental-formative influences	—	22
'Egoistic vs. prosocial'	9	Children assuming the position	45	—
	11	Children not assuming the position	0	—
	3	Children not subjected to the experimental-formative influences	—	100
'Mutual assistance'	8	Children assuming the position	63	—
	0	Children not assuming the position	0	—
	13	Children not subjected to the experimental-formative influences	—	31

pre- and posttests in the 'justice 1' and 'justice 2' situations showed that there were no significant changes in the behaviour of the children after the training session.

As is evident from the results, our expectations were confirmed only partially. To sum up, let us pinpoint a few details.

The fact that in the 'justice 1' and 'justice 2' situations no substantial improvement in the experimental group took place can be interpreted in two ways: either our educational work was unable to alter the children's behaviour in these situations, or these situations were not precise enough to reflect any changes that had taken place in the development of moral motives.

On the other hand, the experimental-formative influences were quite effective: because of them, the positive dynamic in the experimental group exceeded the spontaneous positive dynamic in the control group. Granted, a positive change was obtained only in those children who had actively assumed the position of champion and defender of norms. It was characteristic that only a few more than 50 per cent of the children from this group went over to fulfilling the norm; this result is no better than that obtained in Experiment 1. Children who had not assumed the position of defender of norms continued to break the rules in the control experiments, but among children who had not been subjected to the experimental-formative influences, the level of fulfilment decreased.

This indicated that although, in general, the experimental-formative influences were a rather effective method of inculcating moral behaviour, their influence was local. With regard to such training methods as 'caring for the younger ones' and 'gift giving', they apparently had a positive influence on the emotional atmosphere in the group and made the children's lives more interesting and rich, even increasing the quality of their activities (modelling, drawing, etc.); however, their influence on the moral behaviour of the children was not evident in the control experiments.

Thus, despite the fact that, in general, the overall indices for the experimental group were higher with regard to internal dynamic than were those for the control group and the experimental-formative influences confirmed their effectiveness, the results of the study provide cause for reflection. Why, despite the complexity and length of the training, was its effect so minimal?

This finding can be explained by the fact that although the actual training period was considerably longer than that in the preceding studies, in terms of the number of formative influences per unit of time it was approximately the same; because of the necessarily protracted nature of the experimental-formative influences over time, there was no cumulative effect of these influences. It may be assumed that the formative influences would have been more effective if they had been intensive.

The large number of children who did not assume the position of experimenter's helper in the experimental-formative influences was also perplexing. It may be assumed that a democratic style of social interaction by no means always leads to the child's internal acceptance of the position of champion and defender of norms. Although at the beginning all the children seemed delighted to take on such a role, it may well have happened that many of them only outwardly agreed to play the role of teacher's helper, but did not actually assume that role. This means that these children had not yet acquired the need to assume the social position of an adult (it was on this that our educative method was based), and hence the adult's request for help was not perceived by them as trust or encouragement on the part of the experimenter.

Finally, even the assumption of the position of champion and defender of norm does not always lead to the cultivation of moral motives (Konnikova, 1966, obtained a similar finding in experiments with schoolchildren) or to change in the children's actual behaviour. Despite the fact that such children were pleased to take on the role of defender of norms, this had no impact on their internal attitudes towards themselves and did not create moral self-esteem in them.

Stages of moral development of preschoolers. A general model

The data reported reveal a complex pattern of the ways through which preschool children are engaged in moral behaviour. Basically, three main stages may be distinguished in the development of morality among children.

During the first stage of moral development (from birth to 2 or 2½ years) children have not yet been drawn into the domain of normative moral behaviour to any significant degree. Motivations underlying their behaviours are purely pragmatic (i.e. egocentric). Primary, basic motives (e.g. vital physiological needs, the need for socioemotional contact with adults, etc.) lay the groundwork for the basic forms that the activities of children of these ages encompass. It is through these activities that children assimilate the fundamental structures of social experience: the rhythms and forms of movement, speech, actions with human artifacts, sensory standards of perception, the elementary forms of thought, and so forth. The assimilation of these fundamental tasks gives structure to children's activities. Their behaviour, initially diffused and unorganized, is transformed into a sequence of programmed actions. The structuring of the operational and technical aspects of activities, on the other hand, is also reflected in the motivation underlying the activity since the act of choice implies a coordination and grading of motives.

The first stage of moral (and mental) development is encapsulated in the emergence of two levels (forms) of 'life practice' in the child. These levels have been designated as verbal and actual behaviour. The operational-technical and motivational aspects of behaviour at the verbal level in its fully developed state are such that children's accomplishment of tasks at this level is abstract-alienated (imaginary) in nature. That is, verbal behaviour can occur without impinging on the vital basic needs of the child and at a minimal risk of pragmatic (consequence-based) loss. Technically, verbal tasks may be carried out at this level in the form of linguistic statements, contingent play, figurative activity, imaginative fantasies, and so forth. In reality, only some of these forms of behaviour (e.g. verbal and gestural speech, elementary forms of imaginary play) may appear at this stage of development. However, the children are capable of performing behaviours at the verbal level that they are still incapable of performing at the actual level. These differences in abilities may reflect a lack of some operational or technical abilities necessary to engage in the actual behaviour, or may result from differences in the motivational structures underlying verbal and actual behaviour.

The discordance or discrepancy that exists between verbal and actual behaviour is the major feature of the *second (transitional) stage* of moral development. This stage begins around 2 years of age and lasts through the age of 4, a period that marks the end of infancy and the beginning of the preschool period. During this stage children assimilate moral-normative forms of behaviour for the first time. Initially, these behaviours are learned and performed at the verbal and imaginative levels in the form of rudimentary notions of 'good' and 'bad' and 'must' vs. 'must not'. Some of these notions may exist at the cultural level in the form of discrete demands, duties and socially appropriate behaviours; others, however, may be incorporated in children's consciousness with the behaviour of characters in stories or tales or with sociocultural symbols of normative and antinormative behaviour (for example in Russian culture, 'Vasilisa Prekrasnaya', 'Snow White' and 'Little Red Riding Hood' vs. 'Yaga the Witch', 'Kaschey Immortable' and 'Grey Wolf'). Only later on in development will these primitive ideas be incorporated into conceptions of 'ideal' behaviour and its opposite (e.g. Jakobson and Pocherevina, 1983).

In this stage of moral development, however, children adhere to moral norms only on the verbal level, most often in the forms of statements, judgements and play. Because these norms are socially approved, e.g. reinforced by social controls, children basically have an important motive for observing them. Children's actual behaviour, in contrast, requires a different motivational structure. At this stage of moral development, norms for actual moral behaviour are not yet enforced by rigorous social control. Neither peers nor adults require categorically that children at this stage observe norms for actual moral behaviour and actual behaviour that is contrary to the norms does not lead to serious punishment for children at this stage. Actual moral behaviour (e.g. adherence to the moral norms) requires self-limitation while immoral behaviour may result in a pragmatic advantage. As a result, the behaviour of children at this stage of development who are experiencing actual moral conflict is often contrary to the prevailing moral norm.

The *third stage* of moral development occurs during the middle and late preschool years (from approximately 4 to 7 years of age). During this stage, positive moral norms reveal themselves in children's actual behaviour to a greater extent. However, two distinctive processes underlie this increase: the pragmatic and nonpragmatic modes of behaviour. As a result of these different processes, two relatively distinct lines of actual moral behaviour emerge. These lines of moral behaviour reflect differences between the two types or styles of social interaction and childrearing: authoritarian and democratic styles.

Both observational and experimental studies have shown that the authoritarian and democratic styles of peer–peer and parent–child social interaction coexist, sometimes competing with, and at other times complementing, one another, often within the same family and within the same culture. With age, preschool children's actual moral behaviour increasingly becomes subject to social control by both peers and adults. The forms of such control may vary along a number of dimensions. Children's moral behaviour may be encouraged directly through rewards or discouraged through punishment for immoral behaviour. Other means of social control, such as verbal approval or censure, demonstration of moral behaviour by a personal example, strengthening the pragmatic motivation for moral behaviour by involving the child in diverse forms of play or work activities and social encouragement of moral behaviour by assigning the child to lead a group of children, also may influence children's performance of actual moral behaviour less directly. While these external controls exert their influence on preschool children's actual moral behaviour, internal controls begin to exert influence at later stages of development.

Despite the apparent diversity in the structural features of these external controls on children's moral behaviour they are but variations of the same universal parameters (e.g. degree of mediation, temporal relationships between actions and consequences, nature of encouragements, etc.). As children move into the middle preschool period they become involved in a variety of forms of cooperative behaviour with their peers and are subject to increasingly stringent external control over their moral behaviour. We assume, however, that all of these forms of external control are merely different manifestations of the authoritarian style of social interaction, a style that results in an intensification of external pragmatic motives for moral behaviour. One outcome of this intensified external control of children's behaviour is that diverse forms of pragmatic moral-normative behaviour emerge and are consolidated in the real-life behaviour of children.

The analysis has shown, however, that many types of interaction between children and adults (particularly parents) may include elements of the democratic style of social interaction. This style may display itself through the forgiving of children's misdeeds by adults, through adults' involving the child in their 'serious' activities, through mutual engagement of children and adults in cooperative play, etc. In all these activities the adult deliberately refutes his or her legitimate right to exert unilateral control over the child's behaviour and promotes the child to a social position equal to that of the adult. It is important to recognize, however, that pragmatic and democratic styles of social interaction rarely assume a 'personal embodiment'. Usually, elements of both styles coexist within the interaction style of the same adult (parent, teacher, relative, etc.).

Developmentally, as a result of experiencing democratic styles of social interaction, the idealized notions of morality that exist in children at the verbal level begin to become less alienated from their self-images during the middle of the preschool period. Children begin to perceive (experience) these moral idealized notions as guides for both verbal and actual moral behaviour.

The result of this fusion between idealized- and moral self-images is that the categories of good and evil, which previously existed only as abstract knowledge, now acquire an affective content. This reflexive investiture is not an act of will or reason on the part of the child. Rather, it is profoundly personal and emotional. The need that arises from this investiture to maintain congruity between the self and the idealized moral image is the need for positive moral self-esteem. The emergence of moral self-esteem gives rise, in turn, to the first forms of moral, nonpragmatic behaviour in the child.

In conclusion, it should be noted that the studies reported are the studies of children's moral behaviour and not of their moral judgements. No wonder, therefore, that the results differ substantially from those obtained by Piaget, Kohlberg and their followers. Clearly, even the development of *verbal moral behaviour* in the sense that it has been defined in this book is very unlike the development of moral judgements.

Indeed, most of the stories and dilemmas used to score children's moral judgements were designed in such a way that they could (although with varying success) indirectly tell the researcher about the certain parameters of *moral consciousness* (for instance, about children's tendency to judge peers' offenses in terms of the material damage they caused, or about children's belief in 'immanent justice' or in the 'conventionality' of moral norms, etc.). In contrast, what is meant by verbal moral behaviour is just *children's direct statements about actions of the story characters*: whether they are good or bad, and whether the children would or would not reproduce the behaviour if they were in the place of the story characters. The objective of studying children's verbal behaviour was not, therefore, to determine *certain characteristics of children's moral consciousness* but whether the children knew about this or that moral norm and whether they considered this norm applicable to their own behaviour.

In sum, studying children's verbal moral behaviour does not allow one to build a model of stages of the development of moral consciousness; instead, it allows one to determine at what age the children acquire knowledge about certain moral norms as imperatives for their own behaviour, and how the knowledge acquired influences (or does not influence) the children's real behaviour with respect to the moral norms.

Notes

1.   Of course, each of these moral rules has certain limits beyond which to behave morally would be to act against these rules (for instance, to lie so as not to hurt someone's feelings or even to help a person to die – the extreme case of euthanasia). We will not consider these extreme cases here but will remain in the area of moral behaviour that allows direct application of universal moral rules.
2.   In experimental psychology a moral value of moral and prosocial behaviour is usually referred to as to 'the role of cost' (see, for example, Tipton and Jenkins, 1974; Wagner and Wheeler, 1969).
3.   The study was conducted by the author together with I. V. Kladov-schikova.

Chapter 4

Independent and moral behaviour: diagnostics and development

The major aim of the studies presented in this book was to trace the initial stages of the development of human personality. The history of the term *personality* has been described a number of times (Kon, 1978; Allport, 1938). But the history of the term is not the history of the concept. For centuries, the content we now designate as personality existed and was developed under various terms, in different sciences and even in different spheres of active assimilation of the world. In ancient Greece, philosophy and ethics had a monopoly of this content, and in other historical epochs it was more productively assimilated by art. In the twentieth century, it became the subject of empirical psychological research.

The unique characteristic of the concept of personality compared with other psychological categories consists in the fact that it has always been associated with the very foundations of the conception of the world and human being, with such key concepts as those of freedom, guilt, responsibility, creativity and individuality. This rootedness in historically and culturally variable philosophical categories and in different spheres of assimilation of the world has determined the complex destiny of the concept of personality, its multilevel and multidimensional nature.

This multidimensionality confronts an experimentalist with a hard option: what kind of qualities should be selected for a thorough experimental study of personality? It is reasonable to assume that they must be the qualities that most closely correspond to certain theoretical or practical goals.

Having chosen the development of a socially matured individual as such a goal, I assumed that in European cultures two personality qualities may be viewed as essential for social maturity: they are *independence* and *moral behaviour*. Independence (nonconformity) enables the individual to follow his or her own new ways in thinking and behaviour and to make his or her original contribution in the cultural and social environment, morality prevents the development of the independent individual into a 'superhuman' creature and provides him or her with intrinsic barriers that force the person to respect independence in other people. The studies therefore aimed to determine the psychological structure and the causes of the development of the two mutually additive qualities in preschool- and primary school-age children.

In order to test the development of independent behaviour of young preschoolers 'conflicting programmes' were applied (for instance, the child was asked to lift a toy if the experimenter lifted a flag, and vice-versa, to lift a flag if the experimenter lifted a toy). In the second part of the experiment the same child was asked to reproduce the programme together with a partner. The experimental group was composed of three persons: the experimenter, the child and the partner. The child and the partner sat face to face in order to be able to see each other's actions. Before the experiment the experimenter asked the partner to intermingle right and wrong actions so that the child would not know about it. Therefore, when the child discovered that his or her partner performed a wrong action, he or she had to choose whether to imitate the partner's actions but break the programme (and break his or her indirect 'promise' to fulfil the programme well), or to put him/herself in opposition to the partner by keeping to the correct responses.

There were two independent variables: the type of behaviour (verbal assessment of the partner's actions vs. real actions) and the type of partner (a peer vs. an adult). The results showed that independent behaviour first appears in the domain of verbal judgements and then in the domain of actual deeds. Children first display independence relative to their peers, and then, somewhat later, relative to adults. Comparison of children's verbal behaviours while their partners were performing conflict and nonconflict programmes showed no significant differences in independence, which testifies in favour of the assumption that the cause of global imitation was not the difficulty of the programme itself.

Global imitation in children was particularly salient when the children were asked to fulfil the programmes together with an adult partner. Their errors were so crude that they could hardly be attributed to a lack of basic knowledge or skills. It made me think that these errors had been caused by a new motive – by children's attitude towards an adult as to an 'ideal model' who simply could not do something wrong (GIA). The social position of a young child is really such that an adult usually monopolizes the functions of a leader (teacher and controller), and the child is usually 'a pupil'. Because of that, for the child imitation becomes not only 'a mechanism of learning' but a way of communication with an adult, a way for the child to show his or her 'loyalty' and obedience, e.g. it becomes an autonomous motive of children's behaviour. This 'imitative motive' might have just been the factor that caused the children's conforming reactions. However, this hypothesis does not exclude certain alternative interpretations.

First of all, it can be assumed that in a process of fulfilment a child might forget the programme, so that he or she has no alternative but to imitate a partner's actions. Nevertheless, the control experiment showed that when the partner was excluded from the situation the children immediately returned to the right process. Second, it could be supposed that the children failed to compare the partner's actions with the programme, and therefore did not appreciate the inadequacy of their partner's actions. To test the hypothesis I asked the children to control the partner's actions verbally without taking part in the fulfilment. It was found that the majority of the children could easily tell their partner's right and wrong actions verbally, but when taking part in the real fulfilment they began to imitate again. So, the children imitated the partner despite knowing that he or she was making mistakes.

Finally, it could be assumed that children's global imitation is caused by the immaturity of their voluntary behaviour (see Luria and Subbotsky, 1978). Conflict programmes demand a rather developed level of voluntary behaviour; however, when a child is doing the programme with a partner who is copying the experimenter, this 'voluntary level' could become unsatisfactory because here the child is under pressure of not one, but two challenging perceptual stimuli (i.e. two flags or two toys). To examine this hypothesis the same children were asked to reproduce the same programmes not with an adult but with a peer partner whose behaviour was also a mixture of right and wrong actions. If it was the failure of the child's 'voluntary capacity' that caused his or her conformity to an adult partner, then the same conformity must be demonstrated in relation to a peer partner because the change of partners did not change the cognitive structure of the situation. But if motivational explanation was right and children's conformity was due to their GIA towards the authority, then in the new situation conformity would substantially decrease. The latter indeed took place in the experiment.

So experimental analysis of 'deviations' in children's behaviour made it possible to reduce the intellectualistic interpretations and to show that the deviations were caused by motivation, e.g. by the attitude towards the adult as to an 'infallible ideal'. A further step in analyzing this motivation was to investigate whether it was internally or externally determined: it was necessary to ascertain whether or not this attitude was really an autonomous 'imitative motive', or whether the deviations were the result of self-preservation (the child's fear of sanctions from the partner if the child contradicted him or her). The experiment in which we separated the partners (the partner had been isolated from the child by a screen; he or she could not see the child but the child could see the adult's hands) supported the first hypothesis: for the majority of the children, imitation did not decrease substantially. This means that children's conformity is not the result of a 'pretence' which is evoked by fear of sanctions, but that they really considered all the partner's actions to be right.

Lastly, the motivation of children's independent (nonconforming) behaviour also required a more precise explanation. On the one hand, independence in the experiment could have been motivated pragmatically (e.g. by a desire to be approved by the experimenter for good performances or by fear of his or her disapproval in the case of deviation); on the other hand, children's nonconforming behaviour could have been motivated by self-esteem (e.g. by the child's desire simply to keep to the programme and therefore to maintain his or her competency). The experiments involving separation of the child and the experimenter (the experimenter was isolated from the child and his or her partner by a screen; he or she could not see the child but the child and his or her partner could see the experimenter's actions) strongly supported the second hypothesis.

In a series of intervention studies we tried to overcome the conformative behaviour in children and to facilitate independence. Since there are at least three possible causes that could determine conformity actions in children ((1) underdevelopment of voluntary behaviour, (2) absence of some necessary intellectual skills (ability to keep the programme in active memory, to compare a partner's actions to the programme), and (3) motivation (the GIA towards the partner as to an 'ideal model)), we chose children (of 5 to 7 years old) who were nonconformists while working with a peer partner, but imitated all the actions of an adult partner; they were then distributed in three experimental groups matched in age and sex. In so far as all the subjects possessed the capacity to perform the conflict programmes correctly with a peer partner, it went without saying that they reached the necessary level of voluntary behaviour. Then only the second and the third hypotheses remained to be verified.

According to the second hypothesis, to foster children's independent behaviour in the presence of an adult partner in the standard experimental situation, the children should either be trained to fulfil the programmes (in order to make them more salient), or be helped to become aware of the fact that the adult partner makes mistakes. So in the first experimental condition the children were trained to perform the programmes tête-à-tête with the experimenter. In the second condition the children were taught to correct the actions of the adult partner verbally. In the third condition the positions of the child and his or her adult partner were reversed: the child was asked to teach the programme to the adult partner and to control his or her actions. It was assumed that the change in the child's submissive social position would destroy his or her GIA towards adults and thus facilitate independent behaviour in the child. Control tests revealed that only the third condition yielded positive results. It was concluded therefore that it was just the unilateral social relations between a child and an adult that created a major obstacle for independent behaviour to develop in preschool-age children.

In subsequent experiments designed to examine this hypothesis children were subjected to either an authoritarian or a democratic style of social interaction with adults. The experiments showed that whereas the authoritarian interaction led to a significant increase in children's conforming behaviour, the democratic type of interaction enhanced independent behaviour.

Since an authoritarian type of social relations was a characteristic feature of the education in a classroom, a series of field experiments was conducted in which the unilateral authoritarian style of social interaction was replaced by the democratic style. A special educational programme was worked out. In the process of communication between teachers and children (3- to 5-year-olds) in a kindergarten, the positions of teacher and pupil were reversed. A group of children and two adults took part in these 'lessons', one of the adults acted as a teacher and the other as a child. In the first part of the lesson the children were shown how to produce some material in painting, sculpture, literature, etc. In the second part, one of them reproduced the material while others corrected his or her actions. In the third part, the adult who acted as a child reproduced the same material and made mistakes while the children corrected him and acted as models. Every week the adults changed their roles. Another principle of this educational work was the absence of authoritarian influence including any (even minimal) punishment. The lessons were carried out five times a week for five months.

The method represented an attempt to change from a traditional (at least for the Russian culture) authoritarian to a democratic style of social interaction between adults and children. One of two roles of every real person was played by each of the adults: the role of a 'model for emulation' and the role of 'hesitations, doubts and faults'. Control experiments showed that the number of children revealing independent behaviour in experimental groups increased significantly compared with the control groups. Similar (although less salient) results were yielded when a 'mixed' type of social interaction was employed in which elements of both authoritarian and democratic styles were combined.

The results prompted me to create a hypothesis according to which the development of initial forms of independent behaviour in preschool-age children was portrayed as a consequence of a gradual transition from the predominance of a unilateral authoritarian style in social interaction between children and adults to a democratic style. This style appears with the emergence of cooperative activities in which children and adults are increasingly involved.

A similar experimental approach was applied to the studies of moral behaviour. A distinction between the form and the content of a moral act was made. In terms of form, a moral act was described as either verbal or real behaviour according to moral norms and imperatives. Whereas verbal moral behaviour was viewed as an abstract-alienated judgement by the subject about how he or she should behave in an imaginary situation entailing a moral conflict (i.e. in a situation requiring a choice between an egoistic act and an altruistic act), real moral behaviour was portrayed as an act in which moral norms are observed in a real situation containing a real moral conflict.

For an experimental comparison of verbal and real behaviour, situations of moral conflict were created that were identical in structure but different in form. Thus, in one of the studies, a child was told a story about a boy instructed by an adult to transfer ping-pong balls from a pail into a jar using a special shovel, without touching them with his hands. Unable to cope with the task, the boy took advantage of the adult's absence to transfer the balls by hand and, having thus deceived the adult, received the reward promised him for performing the task correctly. The subject in our experiment was asked to judge the boy's actions and say how he or she would behave in the boy's place. To study a child's real behaviour, the child was placed in a situation analogous to that of the boy in the story (the child was asked to transfer the balls with the shovel and was promised a reward for this; the adult went out of the room, but secretly observed the child's behaviour through a screen).

The results revealed a gap between verbal and real behaviour: significantly more children of 3, 4, 5, 6 and 7 years old upheld moral rules in their verbal judgements than in their real actions without a direct external control. An even smaller number of children revealed moral behaviour after they had witnessed the peer's deviation; the cause for that was assumed to be the elimination of the imaginary external control that earlier may have exerted a certain inhibiting influence upon children's behaviour even if the direct external control was absent. The discrepancy between verbal and real moral behaviour was also observed in other experimental situations.

The comparison between the effects of the peers' and adults' external control on children's behaviour in this 'honesty' situation showed that if the adult's control prevents deviations from moral rules even among 3-year-olds, the peer's control has no effect upon children of this age and gains an inhibiting value only gradually. It was assumed that a certain role in this process might be attributed to social expectations by adults, who gradually start to view children as responsible not only for their own deviations from moral norms but also for the deviations of younger children. A questionnaire completed by the group of parents strongly supported the hypothesis.

At the same time the data showed that a significant number of children in the 'honesty' situation revealed moral behaviour in the absence of both direct and indirect (imaginary) external control. Since this type of moral behaviour could not have been motivated by fear of punishment or by the desire to obtain a reward (a pragmatic moral motivation), it was assumed that it was motivated by the children's desire to maintain their moral self-esteem: to be honest, to uphold moral norms (a motivation of nonpragmatic moral behaviour). The question arose as to what kinds of factors could possibly have caused the appearance of this motivation.

It was assumed that the development of pragmatic and nonpragmatic moral motivation could be satisfactorily explained through the concept of styles of social interaction: whereas a unilateral authoritarian style of social interaction between children and adults exerts its influence upon the children's moral behaviour through various forms of external control, the democratic style enhances a positive self-image in the child and creates a desire 'to be like adults', therefore to uphold moral regulations even in the absence of any external control.

The experiments in which various parenting styles were compared to the children's moral conduct indirectly supported this view. They showed that the children whose parents were inclined to the authoritarian parenting styles mainly revealed pragmatic moral conduct in the 'honesty' situation, whereas the children of parents who favoured the nonauthoritarian styles showed nonpragmatically motivated moral behaviour. The hypothesis that the democratic style of social interaction may enhance children's subsequent moral behaviour gained partial support in the experiments in which children with positive or negative prior experience had an opportunity to share their rewards with peers.

A direct comparison between the effects of various interventional methods showed that the methods containing elements of the democratic style of social interaction did indeed enhance nonpragmatic moral behaviour in children, whereas the methods that involved no such elements did not. An application of various forms of DSI in a field experiment in a classroom yielded less encouraging results since there was no overall improvement in nonpragmatic moral behaviour in the experimental group compared to the control one. Nevertheless, a more thorough analysis did reveal certain differences: in the experimental group substantially more children shifted from deviative behaviour in the pretests to moral behaviour in posttests than in the control group, whereas the opposite dynamic was more salient in the control group.

In sum, in the studies of both independent and moral behaviour, along with many differences, certain common phenomena were registered. Let us examine them more thoroughly.

The first was *a discrepancy between verbal and real behaviour*. This psychological phenomenon has been noted in a number of studies and in our investigations took the following form: a child would assimilate moral norms verbally far in advance of being able to adhere to these norms in a situation of real moral conflict. We found that when discussing the behaviours of the characters in stories, practically all of our subjects demonstrated a firm knowledge of behavioural norms and, moreover, considered them binding on themselves; however, once in a situation of real moral conflict, most of the children deviated from these norms despite their previously stated acceptance of them. It was characteristic that this discrepancy between verbal and real behaviour was markedly unilateral: in planning their behaviour verbally, the children would adhere to socially approved norms; but in the real situation, they would violate them. Cases of discrepancy in the opposite direction (violation of the norms verbally, but observation of them in a real situation) have not been observed.

Although the discrepancy draws upon the phenomenon found and discussed in many other studies (see Arbuthnot, 1975; Kohlberg, 1966; Libby and Garrett, 1974; Piaget, 1954), a direct comparison between the present data and the data obtained in those studies does not seem possible. The position is that the comparison between children's verbal and actual moral behaviour made in this study was based on a strict correspondence between the moral tasks presented in verbal and in real forms. In contrast, in the studies mentioned above verbal and real behaviour were treated differently: in the area of verbal behaviour children's moral consciousness was studied by obtaining moral judgements with respect to various imagined situations, whereas children's real behaviour was measured in real situations that substantially differed from those described in tests on moral judgements (for instance, through measuring children's sharing or helping behaviours in experiments or through teacher's accounts, etc.). As a result, the comparison between children's verbal and real behavioural scores could only be correlational and it was not possible to determine what causes for the discrepancy between the two types of behaviour (if obtained) had emerged: they werre either due to the differences in motivational underpinnings of verbal and real behaviours or to structural differences in the moral tasks involved. In contrast, in our approach structurally identical tasks were employed both in determining children's verbal and their real behaviours and, therefore, a discrepancy between them could only have been the result of differences in their specific motivations.

A completely analogous phenomenon was observed in the study of children's independent behaviour. In almost every age group a considerable number of children were observed who displayed independent behaviour at the verbal level (objective verbal correction of the actions of their partner), but then would go on to copy the mistakes of their partner when they performed the tasks themselves. Cases in which contrary forms of behaviour were engaged in simultaneously were especially conspicuous: after calling a partner's erroneous action wrong, the child would then go on to copy it him/ herself. In this series of experiments, too, this discrepancy was distinctly one-sided: the number of children who displayed independence in actually performing the tasks, but who were unable verbally to control their partner, was insignificant. Finally, in a study of children's value judgements with regard to the qualities of objects, it was found that a considerable number of subjects were able to compare and evaluate the qualities of objects correctly if they did so abstractly, from a distance, but when they were in a situation of competition with a peer (modelling and drawing the same objects), they would say that their work was better, even though it had been deliberately made more poorly, finding in it such 'merits' as would never occur to an independent observer (Subbotsky, 1978b).

As noted earlier, instances of discrepancies between verbal and real behaviour are not a rarity in psychology and pedagogy and there have been a number of attempts to account for the discrepancies (see Chapter 1 above), some of which seem to be relevant to the results obtained in our studies.

As has been noted, a discrepancy between verbal and real behaviour may take many forms. The simplest of these is, for example, the inability to resolve in practice a task that has been resolved theoretically because of certain 'material' limitations, e.g. the absence of necessary means and materials. Psychologically, such a discrepancy will be reflected in the subject's lack of certain skills and abilities (for example, the ability to evaluate the degree of perfection of a gymnast's feats theoretically is not necessarily accompanied by the ability to perform such feats oneself). The reasons for this type of discrepancy between verbal and real behaviour are sufficiently obvious and are of no special interest for our analysis. Much more 'heuristic' is that form which occurs despite the fact that the subject has at his or her disposal all the operational and technical means necessary to carry out 'knowable' normative behaviour.

A special experimental analysis of child behaviour we carried out during the investigations showed that neither the children's violation of moral norms nor 'global imitative' and 'partisan' behaviour can be attributed to the fact that the intelligence and will have not yet developed to the level necessary for correct behaviour in these children. Thus, the reason for these discrepancies is to be found in the motives of our subjects, which undergo a change in the transition from verbal to real behaviour. Initially, it was postulated that, assuming the motivation or aim in both levels (forms) of behaviour was identical, a child might not be able actually to 'achieve' this aim because the operational and technical needs necessary for it were not sufficiently developed in him or her; later, the experimental analysis led me to discard this hypothesis. The hypothesis that remained was that, assuming the child possessed all the necessary operational and technical means for positive normative behaviour, any deviation from the norms in real behaviour would be for motivational reasons. In other words, the reason for a discrepancy between verbal and real behaviour lies in a difference in the 'motivational components' at these levels of behaviour.

In fact, these motivational differences show quite clearly that the way children observe moral norms in a situation of moral conflict, presented to the child in abstract terms, differs from a real conflict in that the former case lacks any motive of importance for the child (a real 'temptation') that would incline him or her to violate the norm; on the other hand, a pragmatic motive for normative behaviour (the desire to be evaluated in positive terms by the experimenter) is quite strong. However, in a real conflict situation, the pragmatic motive for normative behaviour diminishes when there is no external control, at the same time as there now appears a strong motive to violate the norm (the desire to receive a reward for carrying out the assignment).

Similar changes in motivation take place when, after comparing drawings and clay figures 'theoretically', the child then goes on to compare them in a competitive situation; although in this situation the motive of normative behaviour introduced by the experimenter's external control is still present, a significant motive 'to deviate from the norm' (the desire to win) now appears. With respect to independent behaviour, the motivation for verbally correcting a partner and the motivation for actually performing a task at the same time as one's partner also differed: it may be assumed that because a child does not want to contradict an adult partner, the pragmatic 'emulative motive' will be more powerful when a task is actually performed than at the level of verbal behaviour, where such a contradiction is weaker.

Thus, the discrepancy between verbal and real behaviour amounts essentially to a distinction between two domains of a child's practical life, each with operational-technical and motivational components having features specific to it. These features are such that the child is able to assimilate the normative forms of behaviour at the verbal level much more rapidly than at the level of real behaviour. Hence, the genesis of moral behaviour as well as of independent behaviour differs at these two levels (forms) of behaviour, and must be examined separately.

Of course, the descriptive terms *verbal* and *real* for forms of behaviour are, to a certain extent, only conventions. Verbal behaviour is not at all identical with speech or linguistic behaviour. Thus, the value judgement about the qualities of objects may take place at both the verbal (abstract, distant comparison of objects) and the real level (comparison of objects in a competitive situation) even though it takes place in words. Consequently, I call the verbal level of moral behaviour that level in which motives inclining the child to violate norms are either absent or minimal; a second characteristic is that an act is carried out in reflexive form, in the form of a 'planning' act. For this reason verbal behaviour usually coincides with 'speech' behaviour and is a 'judgement about deeds', whereas real behaviour amounts to the accomplishment of these deeds as such.

The second common feature for the development of moral and independent behaviour is that *both of them benefit from the fundamental transition that occurs during the preschool and primary school childhood: the transition from the predominance of the unilateral authoritarian style in social interaction between children and adults to the gradually increasing number of activities based upon the democratic style of social interaction.* This prompts me to assume that, despite all the differences between independent and moral behaviour, they share certain global factors that determine their emergence and development in preschool-age children.

An examination of the empirical findings available in the literature and of those accumulated in the studies described above reveals a quite complex picture for the mental development of the preschool child in which incipient forms of moral and independent behaviour begin to take shape in the child. Forgoing a rigorous chronological periodization, I distinguished three basic stages in this development.

At the *first stage*, the child has not yet been drawn into the domain of normative moral demands to any significant degree. His or her motivation is exclusively pragmatic (egocentric): it involves such powerful and primary basic motives as vital organic needs, the need for emotional contact with adults, the need for external impressions, an explorative need, etc. These primary basic motives, which show up in all their immediacy and force at the very outset, lay the groundwork for the basic forms of activity of a child in this age, during the course of which the child assimilates the fundamental structures of social experience: the rhythm and forms of movements, speech, actions with objects, sensory standards of perception, the elementary forms of thought, etc. This assimilation inevitably takes the shape of global imitation of adults' actions so that imitation embraces all the channels of social interactions between a child and an adult.

The assimilation of these fundamental tasks gives structure to the child's activity: his or her behaviour, at first diffuse and unorganized, is gradually transformed into a sequence of programmed actions, each of which presupposes the selection of a specific act from a number of possible ones. The structuring of the preoperational and technical aspect of activity, on the other hand, is also reflected in its motivation, since an act of choice implies a coordination of motives; the motivation of activity, at first immediate and homogeneous, is broken up into discrete elements, which then take on hierarchical form.

The main content and essence of this stage of mental development amounts, in my view, to the emergence of two levels (forms) of life practice in the child, which I have designated the levels of verbal and real behaviour. As I have said earlier, the operational-technical and motivational aspects of the verbal level of activity in its fully developed state are such that the child's accomplishment of tasks at the verbal level is of an orienting nature, i.e. it can take place without impinging on the vital, basic needs of the child, with a minimal risk of pragmatic loss to him or her. Technically, a task may be carried out at this level at the form of linguistic statements, contingent play actions, figurative activity, pictures in the imagination, etc. – i.e. forms of behaviour only some of which (verbal and gestural speech, the elementary forms of imagination) appear at this stage. Tasks become accessible to the child at the verbal level of life practice, though he or she may still be incapable of performing them at the real level. The child is already able theoretically to 'manoeuvre' with diverse, sometimes contrasting, acts (for example, in judgements he or she can just as easily observe moral norms as diverge from them); the practical performance of these acts, on the other hand, may be hindered for two kinds of reasons.

First (and this has been pointed out a number of times in the literature), while following through with any act (programme) at the verbal level, the child may nonetheless not have the operational and technical means necessary for the act to be accomplished in real behaviour. The coordination of the operational and technical aspects of verbal and real behaviour, i.e. 'orienting' and 'practical' behaviour, is a psychological problem in its own right, which has been dealt with quite thoroughly in psychology (see, for instance, Zaporozhets, 1960). Much less work has been done on that aspect of discrepancy whose causes lie in differences in the motivational structures of verbal and real behaviour, respectively. It is this aspect that, in my view, is of fundamental importance for understanding the development of moral and independent behaviour in children.

Specifically, this particular type of discordance (discrepancy) between verbal and real behaviour is the main feature of the *second (transitional) stage* in the development of moral-normative behaviour in children. In this stage, which marks the end of infancy and beginning of the preschool age, the child assimilates moral norms of behaviour for the first time. These behaviours are initially learned and performed at the verbal level, in the form of elementary notions about good and evil, the good and the bad, must and must not. Some of these notions exist in the form of discrete demands, duties and imperatives of socially approved and socially unapproved behaviour, and some are mingled in the child's consciousness with the behaviour of characters in stories, tales, etc. – i.e. sociocultural symbols of normative and antinormative behaviour. We can also assume that, later, a child will form a concept of an 'ideal model' of behaviour and its antipode on the basis of these notions. In a number of cases these notions (and this concept) may become one in the child's consciousness with the image of some specific (usually an adult) person. This merging of the norms of behaviour and the image of their bearer (an adult) has one more consequence: it makes it particularly difficult for the child to compare the norms and the adults' actions and enhances the child's GIA towards adults. In particular, this may account for the fact obtained in our studies that 3-year-old children could observe moral norms in their verbal judgements; however, a significantly smaller number of the children were able to control verbally the actions of adults who were performing conflict programmes (compare, for instance, Figure 2.5 and Figure 3.2, verbal behaviours).

In this stage, however, the moral norms of behaviour are adhered to by the child only at the verbal level, in the form of statements, judgements, play actions, etc. Since these norms are socially approved, i.e. are reinforced by social control, the child has an important motive for observing them. At the same time, engaging in 'antinormative' forms of behaviour at the verbal level brings no pragmatic advantages to the child, and he or she has no important motivation for deviating from the norms. Hence, it is clear that normative forms of behaviour begin to predominate and occupy a leading position in the verbal domain, while contrary modes of behaviour are relegated to a secondary level, becoming merely potential.

The child's real behaviour acquires another motivational structure. At this level, moral norms usually are not observed by the child if they are not reinforced by rigorous social control. The predominance of the unilateral authoritarian style in social interaction between children and adults determined by the gap between the intellectual and physical abilities of young children and adults, on the one hand, creates no favourable conditions for a moral self-esteem to appear in the child. On the other hand, this predominance enhances the emergence of a GIA towards adults. As a result, *pragmatic moral behaviour and conformity predominate in real actions of children in this stage.*

The chief characteristic of the *third stage* (late preschool age and primary school age) is that the increase of children's intellectual and physical abilities creates an opportunity for them to be involved in cooperative activities with adults. Within these activities a democratic style of social interaction between children and adults first appears. Both observations and experimental studies testify that at this stage the two aforementioned styles of social interaction between a child and his or her peers and adults may actually coexist, sometimes competing with one another, sometimes organically complementing one another, within the same family, social group, or culture as a whole.

On the one hand, a preschool-age child's behaviour is subject to increasing social control from peers and adults as the child becomes older. The forms of such control are varied: direct encouragement or punishment, verbal approval or censure, the demonstration of a personal example, strengthening of a pragmatic motivation for moral behaviour by assigning to the child the functions of a leader of group of children, etc. Despite their external diversity, all these tactics involve external controls differing in only a few parameters (degree of mediation, distance in time between an action and a reinforcement, nature of the reinforcement, etc.). One particular form of the external control may appear through the child's increasing involvement in cooperative activities *with peers*. I assume that all these forms of controls are but different manifestations of a pragmatic style of social interaction and result in an intensification of external pragmatic motives for moral behaviour. One outcome of this intensified external control of a child's behaviour is that diverse forms of pragmatic moral-normative behaviour emerge and are consolidated into the child's real-life practice.

On the other hand, a progressive involvement of the child in cooperative activities *with adults* (mostly with close adults) brings different results. In these activities the unilateral subordination of the child to adults disappears and the child has an opportunity for the first time in his or her life to feel him/herself to be an equal with an adult. This feeling, as it accumulates, cannot but have a dramatic impact on the child's self-image, as well as on the child's image of an adult.

First, it may be assumed that in these activities the child's GIA towards adults is gradually fading and being replaced by a more realistic image of an adult as a person who can make mistakes and experience hesitations and uncertainty. Second, this newly acquired 'proximity' between the child's self-image and the image of an adult person makes the child's original goal 'to be like adults' more accessible and encourages the child's desire to uphold 'adults' ways of behaviour' in certain situations, to which situations of moral conflict belong. This may be the mechanism through which *a positive moral self-esteem develops in a child and early forms of nonpragmatic moral behaviour and independent behaviour emerge in the child in the third stage.*

As it has been pointed out, cooperative activities among children and between children and adults were referred to by many authors, in particular by Piaget in his account of the causes of children's cognitive development (Piaget, 1954, 1977). According to Piaget, such activity makes a substantial contribution towards overcoming children's intellectual and social egocentrism and in the development of logical operations which, in turn, are able to exercise a backward influence upon cooperative activities, thus creating a more favourable ground in which they can flourish. Clearly, cooperative-type activities play a different role in the installation of behaviours studied in this book than the role of overcoming children's egocentrism: their major functions are in increasing the external controls, on the one hand, and in eliminating children's GIA towards adults, on the other hand. In these specific roles cooperative activities begin to function and produce effects on children's behaviours at a significantly earlier age than that outlined by Piaget as the age of operational thinking.

Viewed in this way, independence and nonpragmatic moral behaviour are different yet linked psychological qualities. Whereas pragmatic moral behaviour and global imitativeness (conforming behaviour) flourish in children in the second stage of early personality development and are determined by the 'submissive' social position of a small child relative to adults, nonpragmatic moral behaviour and independence appear as a result of global changes in the child's capacities and of the child's involvement in cooperative activities with adults in the third stage of development. This transition is of a very complex and global nature and has only been touched upon in this book. Nevertheless, it is this transition that, in my view, constitutes the initial and the most important phase in the development of personality.

Of course, both the specific age demarcations of the development of moral and independent behaviour and the rate of their development will vary among children of different social strata, classes, cultures, etc. It is also clear that this development is not limited to the preschool-age period. This period, however, constitutes the most interesting phase for delimiting and analyzing the development of moral and independent behaviour.

Bibliography

Abrams, D., Wetherell, M., Cochrane, S., Hogg, M. and Turner, J. C. (1990), 'Knowing what to think by knowing who you are: self-categorization and the nature of norm formation, conformity and group polarization', *British Journal of Social Psychology*, *29*, 2, 97–119.

Adler, A. (1929), *The Science of Living*, New York: Garden City Publishers.

Adorno, T. W., Frenkel-Brunswik, E., Levinson, D. J. and Sanford, R. N. (1950), *The Authoritarian Personality*, New York: Harper.

Ajzen, I. and Fishbein, M. (1980), *Understanding Attitudes and Predicting Social Behaviour*, Englewood Cliffs, NJ: Prentice-Hall.

Albert, R. S. (1990), 'Real world creativity and eminence: an enduring relationship', *Creativity Research Journal*, *3*, 1, 1–5.

Alexander, F. and Staub, H. (1931), *The Criminal, the Judge and the Public*, Glencoe, (IL): The Free Press.

Allport, G. N. (1938), *Personality*, New York: Holt.

Amato, P. R. and Ochiltree, G. (1986), 'Children becoming independent: an investigation of children's performance of practical life-skills', *Australian Journal of Psychology*, *38*, 1, 56–68.

Ambron, S. R. and Irwin, D. M. (1975), 'Role taking and moral judgment in five- and seven-year-olds', *Developmental Psychology*, *11*, 102–10.

Ames, C. and Ames, R. (eds) (1989), *Research on Motivation in Education, Vol.3. Goals and Cognitions*, San Diego: Academic Press.

Arbuthnot, J. (1975), 'Modification of moral judgement through role playing', *Developmental Psychology*, *11*, 3, 319–24.

Aronfreed, J. (1968), *Conduct and Conscience*, New York and London: Academic Press.

Asch, S. E. (1956), *Studies of Independence and Conformity*, Washington: Psychological Monographs.

Aurora, M., Verma, R. and Agrawal, P. (1985), 'Parent and peer conformity in adolescents: an Indian perspective', *Adolescence*, *20*, 78, 467–78.

Bandura, A. and MacDonald, F. J. (1963), 'Influence of social reinforcement and the behavior of models in shaping children's moral judgments', *Journal of Abnormal and Social Psychology*, *67*, 274–81.

Bandura, A. and Walters, R. H. (1964), *Social Learning and Personality Development*, New York, Toronto and London: Holt.

Barker, R. G. (1965), 'Explorations in psychological ecology', *American Psychologist*, *20*, 1–13.

Barkley, K. L. (1942), 'Development of moral judgement of college students', *Character and Personality*, *10*, 3, 199–272.

Batson, D. S. (1990), 'How social an animal? The human capacity for caring', *American Psychologist*, *45*, 3, 336–46.

Baumrind, D. (1967), 'Child care practices anteceding three patterns of preschool behavior', *Genetic Psychology Monographs*, *75*, 43–88.

Baumrind, D. (1971), 'Current patterns of parental authority', *Developmental Psychology Monographs*, *4*, 1, Part 2.

Berenda, R. W. (1950), *The Influence of the Group on Judgment of Children*, New York: Kings Crown.

Berkowitz, M. and Daniels, L. R. (1964), 'Affecting the salience of the social responsibility norm: effects of past help on the response to dependency relationships', *Journal of Abnormal and Social Psychology*, *68*, 3, 275–81.

Berkowitz, M. W. and Gibbs, J. C. (1985), 'The process of moral conflict resolution and moral development', *New Directions for Child Development*, *29*, 71–84.

Berne, E. (1970), *Games People Play*, Harmondsworth: Penguin Books.

Blum, E. J. and Blum, H. P. (1990), 'The development of autonomy and superego precursors', *International Journal of Psycho-Analysis*, *71*, 4, 585–95.

Bordichenko, E. (1965), 'Ob aktivnosti detej v vospitatelnom protsesse' (The activity level of children in the educational process), *Doshkolnoje Vospitanije*, *8*, 28–30.

Borishevsky, M. I. (1965), 'Osobennosti otnoshenija rebenka k pravilam povedenija v igrovoj situatsii' (Specific elements of the child's attitude towards the rules of conduct in play), *Voprosy Psikhologii*, *4*, 44–55.

Boyes, M. C. and Walker, L. J. (1988), 'Implications of cultural diversity for the universality claims of Kohlberg's theory of moral reasoning', *Human Development*, *31*, 1, 44–59.

Bozhovitch, L. I. (1968), *Lichnost i ejo phormirovanije v detskom vozraste* (The personality and its formation in childhood), Moscow: Pedagogica Publications.

Bronfenbrenner, U. (1970), *Two Worlds of Childhood: U.S. and U.S.S.R.*, Newbury Park, CA: Sage.

Bruner, J. S. (1973), *Beyond the Information Given. Studies in the Psychology of Knowing*, New York: W. W. Norton.

Bryan, J. H. (1971), 'Model effect and children's imitative altruism', *Child Development*, *42*, 6, 2061–5.

Bryan, J. H. and Walbek, N. H. (1970a), 'Preaching and practising generosity: children's actions and reactions', *Child Development*, *41*, 2, 329–53.

Bryan J. H. and Walbek, N. (1970b), 'The impact of words and deeds concerning altruism upon children', *Child Development*, *41*, 3, 747–57.

Buck, L. Z., Walsh, W. F. and Rothman, G. (1981), 'Relationship between parental moral judgment and socialization', *Youth and Society*, *13*, 91–116.

Campbell, J. D. and Fairey, P. J. (1989), 'Informational and normative routes to conformity: the effect of faction size as a function of norm extremity and attention to the stimulus', *Journal of Personality & Social Psychology*, *57*, 3, 457–68.

Camus, A. (1942), *Le Mythe de Sisyph*, Paris: Gallimard.

Cattel, R. B. (1957), *Personality and Motivation Structure and Measurement*, New York: World Book Company.

Cole, M. and Cole, S. R. (1989), *The Development of Children*, San Diego: Scientific American Books.

Constanzo, P. R. (1970), 'Conformity development as a function of self-blame', *Journal of Personality and Social Psychology*, *14*, 366–76.

Constanzo, P. R. and Shaw, M. E. (1966), 'Conformity as a function of age level', *Child Development*, *37*, 967–75.

Cook, S. and Selltiz, C. (1964), 'A multiple-indicator approach to attitude measurement', *Psychological Bulletin*, *62*, 36–55.

Corey, S. M. (1937), 'Professed attitudes and actual behaviour', *Journal of Educational Psychology*, *38*, 271–80.

Crittenden, P. M. (1990), 'Toward a concept of autonomy in adolescents with a disability', *Children's Health Care*, *19*, 3, 162–8.

Crockenberg, S. and Litman, C. (1990), 'Autonomy as competence in 2-year-olds: maternal correlates of child defiance, compliance, and self-assertion', *Developmental Psychology*, *26*, 6, 961–71.

Damon, W. (1975), 'Early conceptions of positive justice as related to the development of logical operations', *Child Development*, *46*, 301–12.

Damon, W. (1981), 'The development of justice and self-interest change in childhood', in M. J. Lerner and S. Lerner (eds), *The Justice Motives in Social Behaviour*, New York: Plenum.

Darley, J. M. and Shultz, T. R. (1990), 'Moral rules: their content and acquisition', *Annual Review of Psychology*, *41*, 525–56.

DePalma, D. J. and Foley, J. M. (1975), *Moral Development: Current theory and research*, Hillsdale, NJ: Erlbaum.

Deutsch, M. (1949), 'The directions of behaviour: a field-theoretical approach to the understanding of inconsistencies', *Journal of Social Issues, 5*, 43–9.

Deutsch, M. and Gerard, H. B. (1955), 'A study of normative and informational judgement', *Journal of Abnormal & Social Psychology, 51*, 629–36.

Dollard, J. (1949), 'Under what conditions do opinions predict behaviour?', *Public Opinion Quarterly, 12*, 623–32.

Dunne, J. and Munn, P. (1987), 'Development of justification in disputes with mother and sibling', *Developmental Psychology, 23*, 791–8.

Dunton, K. J. (1989), 'Parental practices associated with their children's moral reasoning development' (Doctoral dissertation, Stanford University, 1988), *Dissertational Abstract International, 49*, 3306A.

Durkin, D. (1959) 'Children's concept of justice: a further comparison with Piaget data', *Journal of Educational Research, 52*, 7, 252–7.

Edwards, C. P. (1980), 'The development of moral reasoning in cross-cultural perspective', in R. H. Munroe, R. L. Munroe and B. B. Whiting (eds), *Handbook of Cross-Cultural Human Development*, New York: Garland Press.

Edwards, C. P. (1982), 'Moral development in comparative cultural perspective', in D. Wagner and H. Stevenson (eds), *Cultural Perspectives on Child Development*, New York: W. H. Freeman.

Edwards, C. P. (1987), 'Culture and the construction of moral values. A comparative ethnography of moral encounters in two cultural settings', in J. Kagan and S. Lamb (eds), *The Emergence of Morality in Young Children*, Chicago: University of Chicago Press, pp. 123–51.

Eisenberg, N. and Miller, P. A. (1987), 'The relation of empathy to prosocial and related behaviours', *Psychological Bulletin, 101*, 1, 91–119.

Eisenberg, N. and Shell, R. (1986), 'Prosocial moral judgment and behaviour in children: the mediating role of cost', *Personality and Social Psychology Bulletin, 12*, 4, 426–33.

Eisenberg, N., Shell, K., Pasternak, J., Lennon, R., Beller, R. and Mathy, R. (1987), 'Prosocial development in middle childhood: a longitudinal study', *Developmental Psychology, 23*, 5, 712–18.

Eisenberg-Berg, N. and Lennon, R. (1980), 'Altruism and the assessment of empathy in preschool years', *Child Development, 51*, 2, 522–57.

El'konin, D. B. (1960), *Detskaja psikchologija* (Child psychology), Moscow: Uchpedgiz Publications.

El'konin, D. B. (1978), *Psikchologija igry* (The psychology of play), Moscow: Pedagogica Publications.

Enright, R. D., Enright, W. F., Mannheim, L. and Harris, B. E. (1980), 'Distributive justice development and social class', *Developmental Psychology, 6*, 555–63.

Erikson, E. (1980), *Identity and Life Cycle*, New York: W. W. Norton.

Eysenk, A. J. (1960), 'The development of moral values in children: the contribution of learning theory', *The British Journal of Educational Psychology*, *30*, 1, 11–21.

Eysenk, A. J. (1970), *The Structure of Human Personality*, London: Methuen.

Ferguson, T. J. and Rule, B. G. (1983), 'An attributional perspective of anger and aggression', in R. G. Green and E. I. Donnerstein (eds), *Aggression: Theoretical and empirical reviews*, New York: Academic Press.

Fichte, J. G. (1956), *The Vocation of Man*, New York: Bobbs-Merrill.

Fishbein, M. (1971), 'Attitude and the prediction of behaviour', in K. Thomas (ed.), *Attitudes and Behaviour*, Baltimore: Penguin Books.

Freedman, J. L. and Wallington, S. A. (1967), 'Compliance without pressure: the effect of guilt', *Journal of Personality and Social Psychology*, *7*, 2, 117–24.

Freeman, L. C. and Aatov, T. (1960), 'Invalidity of indirect and direct measures of attitude towards cheating', *Journal of Personality*, *38*, 443–7.

Freud, A. (1965), *A Normality and Pathology in Childhood*, New York: International University Press.

Freud, S. (1910), *(Psychopathology of everyday life)*, Moscow: Sovremennyje Problemy.

Freud, S. (1966), *Introductory Lectures on Psychoanalysis*, New York: Liveright Publishers Co.

Fromm, E. (1941), *Escape from Freedom*, New York: Farrar and Rinehart.

Fromm, E. (1961), *The Fear of Freedom*, London: Routledge and Kegan Paul.

Gabennesch, H. (1990), 'The perception of social conventionality by children and adults', *Child Development*, *61*, 6, 2047–59.

Gardner, H. (1988), 'Creativity: an interdisciplinary perspective', *Creativity Research Journal*, *1*, 8–26.

Garrison, K. C. (1968), *The Psychology of Childhood. A survey of development and socialization*, London: Staples Press.

Glover, R. J. and Steele, C. (1990), 'Applying neopiagetian theory to the moral reasoning process', *Psychological Reports*, *66*, 3, 1259–72.

Goffman, E. (1982), *The Presentation of Self in Everyday Life*, New York: Penguin Books.

Greenglass, E. R. (1969), 'Effects of prior help and hindrance on willingness to help another: reciprocity or social responsibility?', *Journal of Personality & Social Psychology*, *11*, 3, 224–31.

Hamm, N. H. (1970), 'A partial test of a social learning theory of children's conformity', *Journal of Experimental Child Psychology*, *9*, 1, 29–43.

Hamm, N. H. and Hoving, K. L. (1969), 'Conformity of children in an ambiguous perceptual situation', *Child Development*, *40*, 773–84.

Hamm, N. H. and Hoving, K. L. (1970), 'Conformity in children as a function of grade level and real versus hypothetical adult and peer models', *Journal of Genetic Psychology*, *118*, 2, 253–63.

Hardeman, M. (1972), 'Children's moral reasoning', *The Journal of Genetic Psychology*, *120*, 49–59.

Harré, R. (1979), *Social Being. A Theory for Social Psychology*, Oxford: Basil Blackwell.

Harris, M. B. (1970), 'Reciprocity and generosity: some determinants of sharing in children', *Child Development*, *41*, 2, 313–28.

Harris, M. B., Liquori, R. and Joniak, A. (1973), 'Aggression, altruism, and models', *Journal of Social Psychology*, *91*, 2, 343–4.

Harris, M. B. and Samerott, G. (1975), 'The effects of aggressive and altruistic modelling on subsequent behaviour', *Journal of Social Psychology*, *95*, 2, 173–82.

Hart, D. (1988), 'A longitudinal study of adolescents' socialization and identification as predictors of adult moral judgment development', *Merrill-Palmer Quarterly*, *34*, 245–60.

Heckhausen, H. (1986), *Motivation and Activity*, Part 1. Moscow: Pedagogica Publications.

Helkama, K. (1987), 'Observations on Soviet studies of morality', *Psykologia. Journal of the Finnish Psychological Society*, *22*, 1, 3–12.

Helkama, K. and Ikonen, M. (1986), 'Some correlates of maturity of moral reasoning in Finland', *Behaviour Science Research*, *20*, 1–4, 110–31.

Henry, W. E. (1960), 'Projective techniques', in P. H. Mussen (ed.), *Handbook of Research Methods in Child Development*, New York and London: Wiley.

Hoffman, M. L. (1975), 'Developmental synthesis of affect and cognition and its implications for altruistic motivation', *Developmental Psychology*, *11*, 607–22.

Hoffman, M. L. (1983), 'Empathy, guilt, and social cognition', in W. F. Overton (ed.), *The Relationship between Social and Cognitive Development*, Hillsdale, NJ and London: Erlbaum, pp. 1–51.

Hoffman, M. L. (1988), 'Moral development', in M. H. Bornstein, and M. E. Lamb (eds), *Developmental Psychology: An advanced textbook*, 2nd edn. Hillsdale, NJ and London: Erlbaum.

Hoffman, M. L. and Saltzstein, H. D. (1967), 'Parent discipline and the child's moral development', *Journal of Personality and Social Psychology*, *5*, 45–57.

Holstein, C. B. (1972), 'The relation of children's moral judgment level to that of their parents and to communication patterns in the family', in R. C. Smart and M. S. Smart (eds), *Reading in Child Development and Relationships*, New York: Macmillan, pp. 484–94.

Hook, J. G. and Cook, T. D. (1979), 'Equity theory and the cognitive ability of children', *Psychological Bulletin*, *86*, 429–45.

Horney, K. (1950), *Neurosis and Human Growth*, New York: W. W. Norton.

Hyman, H. (1949), 'Inconsistencies as a problem in attitude measurement', *Journal of Social Issues*, 5, 38–42.

Ilienkov, E. (1979), 'Chto zhe takoje litchnost?' (What is personality?), in R. I. Kosolapov (ed.), *S chego nachinaetsa litchnost* (What personality starts from), Moscow: Politisdat, pp. 183–237.

Isaksen, S. G. and Murdock, M. C. (1990), 'The outlook for the study of creativity: an emerging discipline?', *Studia Psychologica*, 32, 53–79.

Iscoe, J., Williams, M. and Harvey, I. (1963), 'Modification of children's judgments by a stimulated group technique: a normative developmental study', *Child Development*, 34, 963–73.

Iscoe, J., Williams, M., and Harvey, I. (1964), 'Age, intelligence and sex as variables in the conformity behaviour of negro and white children', *Child Development*, 35, 451–60.

Jakobson, S. G. and Pocherevina, L. P. (1983), 'The role of subjective attitude toward ethical models in the regulation of preschoolers' moral conduct', *Soviet Psychology*, 22, 20–37.

Jose, P. E. (1990), 'Just-world reasoning in children's immanent-justice judgments', *Child Development*, 61, 4, 1024–33.

Kant, I. (1965a), (Works), in 6 vols, Vol. 3. Moscow: Mysl'.

Kant, I. (1965b), (*The foundations of the metaphysics of morals*), quoted from the Russian language edition (Works), Vol. 4, Moscow: Mysl' Publications.

Kardiner, A. (1946), '*The Psychological Frontiers of Society*, New York: Columbia University Press.

Karniol, R. (1978), 'Children's use of intention cues in evaluating behaviour', *Psychological Bulletin*, 85, 76–85.

Kay, A. W. (1969), *Moral Development*, New York: Schocken Books.

Knudson, K. H. and Kagan, S. (1982), 'Differential development of empathy and prosocial behavior', *Journal of Genetic Psychology*, 140, 2, 249–51.

Kohlberg, L. (1966), 'The developmental approach to moralization: relationships between maturity of moral judgements and moral conduct', in XVIII *International Congress of Psychology, Symposium 35*, 19–21.

Kohlberg, L. (1969), 'Stage and sequence: The cognitive-developmental approach to socialization', in D. A. Goslin (ed.), *Handbook of Socialization Theory and Research*, Chicago: Rand McNally.

Kohlberg, L. (1976), 'Moral stage and moralization: the cognitive-developmental approach', in T. Lickona (ed.), *Moral Development and Behavior: Theory, research, and social issues*, New York: Holt, Rinehart and Winston, pp. 31–53.

Kohlberg, L. (1984), *The Psychology of Moral Development: The nature and validity of moral stages, (Vol. 2)*, New York: Harper and Row.

Kohlberg, L. and Kramer, R. (1969), 'Continuities and discontinuities in childhood and adult moral development', *Human Development*, 12, 93–120.

Kon, I. S. (1978), *Otkrytije ja* (The discovery of the self), Moscow: Politizdat.

Konnikova, T. E. (1966), 'Rol kollektiva v formirovaniji litchnosti rebenka' (The role of the collective in the formation of the child's personality), in (*Proceedings of the 28th International Psychological Congress. Symposium 35*) Moscow, 50–9.

Kumar, J. (1983), 'Conformity behaviour as a function of confederates' age and size of the confederate group', *Personality Study and Group Behaviour*, *3*, 2, 69–73.

Lacan, J. (1979), *The Four Fundamental Concepts of Psychoanalysis*, New York: Penguin Books.

LaPiere, R. T. (1934), 'Attitudes versus actions', *Social Forces*, *13*, 230–37.

Lennon, R., Eisenberg, N. and Carroll, J. (1986), 'The relation between nonverbal indices of empathy and preschoolers' prosocial behavior', *Journal of Applied Developmental Psychology*, *7*, 3, 219–24.

Leontiev, A. N. (1977), *Dejatelnost. Soznanije. Litchnost* (Activity. Consciousness. Personality), Moscow: Politizdat.

Lepper, M. R. (1983), 'Extrinsic reward and intrinsic motivation: implications for the classroom', in I. M. Levine and M. C. Wang (eds), *Teacher and Student Perceptions* (pp. 281–317), Hillsdale, NJ: Erlbaum.

Lerner, E. (1938), *Observations sur le raisonnement morale de l'enfant*, Geneva: Palais Wilson.

Lerner, M. J. (1974), 'The justice motive: "equity" and "parity" among children', *Journal of Personality and Social Psychology*, *29*, 4, 539–50.

Lewin, K. (1935), *A Dynamic Theory of Personality*, New York and London: McGraw-Hill.

Libby, W. L. and Garrett, J. (1974), 'Role of intentionality in mediating children's responses to inequity', *Developmental Psychology*, *10*, 2, 294–304.

Likona, T. (1976), *Moral Development and Behaviour. Theory, Research and Social Issues*, New York: Holt.

Linton, R. (1959), *Le Fundament culturel de la personalité*, Paris: Dunod.

Lisina, M. I. (1986), *Problemy ontogeneza obschenija* (Problems of the ontogenesis of communication), Moscow: Pedagogica.

Losev, A. F. (1978), *Estetika Vosrozhdenija* (Aesthetics of the Renaissance), Moscow: Mysl Publications.

Loughran, R.A. (1957), 'A pattern of development of moral judgements made by adolescents derived from Piaget's schema of its development in childhood', *Educational Review*, *19*, 79–98.

Luria, A. R. (1971), *Mozg cheloveka i psikhicheskie prozessy* (Human brain and psychological processes), Vol. 2, Moscow: Pedagogica.

Luria, A. R. and Subbotsky, E. V. (1978), 'Zur frühen Ontogeneze der steuerden Funktion der Sprache', in: *Die Psychologie des 20 Jahrhunderts*, Zürich: Kinder Verlag, pp. 1032–48.

Maccoby, E. E. (1980), *Social Development. Psychological Growth and the Parent–Child Relationship*, New York: Harcourt Brace.

Maccoby, E. E. and Martin, J. A. (1983), 'Socialization in the context of the family: parent–child interaction', in P. H. Mussen (ed.), *Handbook of Child Psychology* (4th edn, Vol. 4), New York: Wiley.

Maqsud, M. and Rouhani, S. (1990), 'Self–concept and moral reasoning among Botswana adolescents', *Journal of Social Psychology*, *130*, 6, 829–30.

Maslow, A. H. (1943), 'The authoritarian character structure', *Journal of Social Psychology*, *18*, 401–11.

Maslow, A. H. (1954), *Motivation and Personality*, New York: Harper.

May, R. (ed.) (1969), *Existential psychology*, New York: Random House.

McNemar, Q. (1946), 'Opinion-attitude methodology', *Psychological Bulletin*, *43*, 289–374.

Mead, M. (1963), *Coming of Age in Samoa*, New York: A Mentor Book.

Mead, M. (1970), *Culture and Commitment*, New York: Natural History Press.

Mishel, W. (1968), *Personality and Assessment*, New York: Wiley.

Moreno, J. L. (1946), *Psychodrama, Vol. 1*, New York: Beacon House.

Mowrer, O. H. (1950), *Learning Theory and Personality Dynamics*, New York: Ronald Press.

Mukhina, V. S. (1969), *Bliznetsy* (Twins), Moscow: Prosveschenije Publications.

Mussen, P. H., Conger, I. and Kagan, I. (1979), *Child Development and Personality*, New York, Philadelphia, San Francisco and London: Harper & Row.

Nucci, L. (1985), 'Social conflicts and the development of children's moral and conventional concepts', *New Directions for Child Development*, *29*, 55–70.

Onuf, N. G. (1987), 'Rules and moral development', *Human Development*, *30*, 5, 257–67.

Parikh, B. (1980), 'Development of moral judgment and its relation to family environmental factors in Indian and American families', *Child Development*, *51*, 1030–9.

Penner, A. L. and Davis, H. I. (1969), 'Conformity and the "rational" use of unanimous majority', *Journal of Social Psychology*, *78*, 2, 299–300.

Piaget, J. (1954), *Les Relations entre l'affectivité et l'intelligence dans l'développement mentale de l'enfant*, Paris: Sorbonne.

Piaget, J. (1957), *De Judgement moral chez l'enfant*, Paris: Press Université de France.

Piaget, J. (1977), *Les Operations logiques et la vie sociale*, in *Etudes Sociologiques*, Geneva: Librairie Droz, pp. 143–71.

Pozar, L. and Subbotsky, E. (1984), 'Experimentálny vyskum niekotorych moralnych cért osobnosti deti' (An experimental study of some moral characteristics in children), *Zbornik katedry specialnej a liecebnej pedagogiky, Pedagogickey Fakulty, Univerzity Komenskeho, X*, pp. 9–20.

Prawat, R. S. and Nickerson, J. R. (1985), 'The relationship between teacher thought and action and student affective outcomes', *The Elementary School Journal, 85,* 529–40.

Rabin, A. J. (ed.) (1986), *Projective Techniques for Adolescents and Children*, New York: Springer.

Raush, H. L., Dittman, A. T. and Taylor, T. J. (1959), 'Person, setting and change in social interaction', *Human Relations, 12,* 361–78.

Raush, H. L., Farbman, I. and Llewellyn, L. G. (1960), 'Person, setting and change in social interaction, II. A normal–control study', *Human Relations, 13,* 305–32.

Roe, K. V. (1980), 'Early empathy development in children and the subsequent internalization of moral values', *Journal of Social Psychology, 110,* 1, 147–8.

Rokeach, M. (1960), *The Open and Closed Mind*, New York: Basic Books.

Rosenberg, M. J. and Hovland, C. I. (1960), 'Cognitive, affective, and behavioural components of attitudes', in C. I. Hovland and M. J. Rosenberg (eds), *Attitude, Organization and Change*. New Haven: Yale University Press, pp. 1–14.

Rushton, J. P. (1976), 'Socialization and the altruistic behaviour of children', *Psychological Bulletin, 83,* 898–913.

Rushton, J. P. (1980), *Altruism, Socialization and Society*, Englewood Cliffs, NJ: Prentice Hall.

Sartre, J. P. (1957), *Existentialism and Human Emotions*, New York: Philosophical Library.

Sartre, J. P. (1966), *Of Human Freedom*, New York: Philosophical Library.

Sears, R. R., Maccoby, E. E. and Lewin, H. (1957), *Patterns of Child Rearing*, Evanston, IL: Raw, Peterson.

Sears, R. R., Rau, L. and Alpert, R. (1965), *Identification and Child Rearing*, Stanford, CA: Stanford University Press.

Serow, R. C. and Solomon, D. (1979), 'Classroom climates and students' intergroup behaviour', *Journal of Educational Psychology, 71,* 669–76.

Shweder, R. A., Mahapatra, M. and Miller, J. G. (1987), 'Culture and moral development', in J. Kagan and S. Lamb (eds), *The Emergence of Morality in Young Children*, Chicago: University of Chicago Press, pp. 1–90.

Singh, R. B. and Sharma, S. K. (1989), 'Anxiety and conformity behaviour', *Indian Journal of Current Psychological Research, 4,* 2, 98–102

Skinner, B. F. (1971), *Beyond Freedom and Dignity*, New York, Toronto and London: Bantam and Vintage Books.

Smith, A. (1966), *The Theory of Moral Sentiments*, New York: Kelley.

Solomon, D., Watson, M. S., Delucchi, K. L., Scharps, E. and Battistich, V.

(1988), 'Enhancing children's prosocial behaviour in the classroom', *American Educational Research Journal*, *25*, 4, 527–54.

Staub, E. (1971), 'The use of role playing and induction in children's learning of helping and sharing behaviour', *Child Development*, *42*, 3, 805–16.

Staub, E. (ed.) (1984), *The Development and Maintenance of Prosocial Behaviour: International perspectives on positive morality*, New York: Plenum.

Sternlieb, J. L. and Youniss, J. (1975), 'Moral judgments one year after intentional or consequence modeling', *Journal of Personality and Social Psychology*, *31*, 895-7.

Subbotsky, E. V. (1976), *Psikchologija otnoshenij partnerstva u doshkolnikov* (The psychology of partnership relations in preschool-age children), Moscow: Moscow University Publications.

Subbotsky, E. V. (1978a), 'Genesis moralnogo povedenija u doshkolnikov' (The genesis of moral behaviour in preschool-age children), *Vestniky Moskovskogo Universiteta, Series 14, Psykchologija*, *3*, 13–25.

Subbotsky, E. V. (1978b), 'O pristrastnosti detskogo suzhdenija' (Bias in children's judgements), *Voprosy Psikchologii*, *2*, 81–90.

Subbotsky, E. V. (1979a), 'Phormorovanije moralnogo dejstvija u rebenka' (Shaping moral action in children), *Voprosy Psikchologii*, *3*, 47–55 (see *Soviet Psychology*, *1983*, *22*, 1, 56–71, for English version).

Subbotsky, E. V. (1979b), 'Phormirovanije elementov altruistitcheskogo povedenija u doshkolnikov' (The development of the elements of altruistic behaviour in preschool-age children), *Vestnik Moscovskogo Universiteta, Series 14, Psikchologija*, *2*, 36–47.

Subbotsky, E. V. (1981a), 'Genezis litchnostnogo povedenija u doshkolnikov i styl obschenija' (Communicative style and the genesis of personality in preschoolers), *Voprosy Psikchologii*, *2*, 68–78 (see *Soviet Psychology*, *1987*, *25*, 4, 38–58, for English version).

Subbotsky, E. V. (1981b), 'Phormirovanije moralnogo povedenija u doshkolnokov v uslovijach psikchologo-pedagogicheskogo eksperimenta' (Development of moral behaviour in preschoolers in a psychological-pedagogical experiment), *Vestnik Moskovskogo Universiteta, Series 14, Psikchologija*, *2*, 56–65 (see *Soviet Psychology*, *1981*, *20*, 1, 62–80, for English version).

Subbotsky, E. V. (1983a), 'Nravstvennoje razvitije doshkolnika' (The moral development of the preschool child), *Voprosy Psikchologii*, *4*, 29–38 (see *Soviet Psychology*, *1984*, *22*, 3, 3–19, for English version).

Subbotsky, E. V. (1983b), *Problemy genesisa litchnosti* (The problems of personality genesis), Moscow: VINITI Publications.

Subbotsky, E. V. (1987), 'Litchnost. Tree aspecta issledovanija' (The personality. Three aspects of investigation), *Vestnik Moskovskogo Universit-*

eta, Series 14, Psikchologija, 3, 3–17 (see *Soviet Psychology, 1989, 27,* 4, 25–50, for English version).

Subbotsky, E. V. (in print), 'The formation of independent behaviour in preschoolers: an experimental analysis of conformity and independence', *International Journal of Behavioral Development.*

Subbotsky, E. V., and Drobotova, E. V. (1980), 'Vlijanije stylija obschenija na phormirovanije nezavisimogo povedenija u doshkolnikov' (The impact of the communicative style on the development of the independent behaviour in preschoolers)' in *Novyje Issledovanija v Psikchologii (New Research in Psychology), 2,* 36–42.

Sullivan, H. S. (1953), *The Interpersonal Theory of Psychiatry,* New York: W. W. Norton.

Tegano, D. W. and Moran, J. D. (1989), 'Sex differences in the original thinking of preschool and elementary school children', *Creativity Research Journal, 2,* 102–10.

Tietjen, A. M. and Walker, L. J. (1985), 'Moral reasoning and leadership among men in Papua New Guinea society', *Child Development, 21,* 982–92.

Tipton, R. M. and Jenkins, L. (1974), 'Altruism as a function of response cost to the benefactor', *Journal of Psychology, 86,* 2, 209–16.

Tittle, C. R. and Hill, R. J. (1971), 'Attitude measurement and prediction of behaviour: an evaluation of conditions and measurement techniques', in K. Thomas (ed.), *Attitudes and Behaviour,* Baltimore: Penguin Books, pp. 179–95.

Utech, D. A. and Hoving, K. L. (1969), 'Parents and peers as competing influences in the decisions of children of differing ages', *Journal of Social Psychology, 78,* 267–74.

Vanderwiele, M. and D'Hondt, W. (1983), 'How conformist Senegalese adolescents consider themselves to be', *Journal of Adolescence, 6,* 1, 87–92.

Varga, A. J. (1986), *Struktura i tipy roditelskogo otnoshenija* (The structure and types of parental attitude), Moscow: Dissertation Cand. Sci. (Moscow University, Department of Psychology).

Vygotsky, L. S. (1987), *Thinking and speech,* in *The Collected Works of L. S. Vygotsky, Vol. 1,* New York: Plenum.

Wagner, C. and Wheeler, L. (1969), 'Model, need, and cost effects in helping behavior', *Journal of Personality and Social Psychology, 12,* 2, 111–16.

Walker, L. J. and Taylor, J. H. (1991), 'Family interactions and the development of moral reasoning', *Child Development, 62,* 2, 264–83.

Wallace, J. and Sadalla, E. (1966), 'Behavioral consequences of transgression: 1. The effect of social recognition', *Journal of Experimental Research in Personality, 1,* 3, 187–94.

Warner, L. G. and DeFleur, M. L. (1969), 'Attitude as an interactional concept: social constraint and social distance as intervening variables between attitudes and action', *American Sociological Review, 34,* 153–69.

Whiting, B. B. and Edwards, C. P. (1988), *Children of Different Worlds*, Cambridge, MA: Harvard University Press.

Whiting, B. B. and Whiting, J. W. M. (1975), *Children of Six Cultures*, Cambridge, MA: Harvard University Press.

Wicker, A. W. (1971), 'Attitudes versus actions: the relationships of verbal and overt behavioural responses to attitude objects', in K. Thomas (ed.), *Attitudes and Behaviour*, Baltimore: Penguin Books.

Yarrow, M. R., Scott, P. M. and Waxler, C. Z. (1973), 'Learning concern for others', *Developmental Psychology*, 8, 2, 240–60.

Zaporozhets, A. V. (1960), *Razvitije proizvolnych dvigenij* (The development of voluntary movements), Moscow: Academy of Pedagogical Sciences Publications.

Name index

Subject index